Ritu Menon is a publisher and writer, and co-founder of the feminist press, Kali for Women. Among her many published books are the ground-breaking *Borders & Boundaries: Women in India's Partition* and *Out of Line: A Literary and Political Biography of Nayantara Sahgal*. She has also edited several anthologies of fiction and non-fiction writing by women.

Also by Ritu Menon

Out of Line: A Literary and Political Biography of Nayantara Sahgal (2014)

Making a Difference: Memoirs from the Women's Movement in India (Ed.) (2010)

No Woman's Land: Women from Pakistan, India & Bangladesh Write on the Partition of India (Ed.) (2004)

Unequal Citizens: A Study of Muslim Women in India (Co-author) (2004)

Borders & Boundaries: Women in India's Partition (1998)

Loitering with INTENT

Diary of a Happy Traveller

Ritu Menon

Illustrated by
A.G. KRISHNA MENON

SPEAKING TIGER

SPEAKING TIGER PUBLISHING PVT. LTD
4381/4 Ansari Road, Daryaganj,
New Delhi–110002, India

First published in India in paperback by Speaking Tiger 2016

Copyright © Ritu Menon 2016

Illustrations copyright © A.G. Krishna Menon

ISBN: 978-93-86050-15-1
eISBN: 978-93-86050-85-4

10 9 8 7 6 5 4 3 2 1

Typeset in Adobe Garamond Pro by SŪRYA, New Delhi
Printed at Gopsons Papers Ltd., Nioda

All rights reserved.
No part of this publication may be reproduced, transmitted, or stored in a retrieval system, in any form or by any means, electronic, mechanical, photocopying, recording or otherwise, without the prior permission of the publisher.

This book is sold subject to the condition that it shall not, by way of trade or otherwise, be lent, resold, hired out, or otherwise circulated, without the publisher's prior consent, in any form of binding or cover other than that in which it is published.

For Bunny
for all the wonderful trips we made together

Contents

Preface	ix
Myanmar Days *February 2012*	1
Cambodia: The Buddhas of Bayon *January 2005*	13
Borobodur and Bali: 'Maybe Later?' *July 2007*	29
Egypt: Revolution in an Ancient Land *November 2011*	51
Turkey: Loitering with Intent *June 2015*	79
Lebanon and Syria: The Lure of the Levant *April–May 2009*	113
Palestine: Grace Under Repression *May 2010*	139
Sicily: Lampedusa Land *September 2012*	163

Bergerac and the Dordogne Valley: 183
Wine, More Wine—and Noble Rot
June 2005

England: Gardens and Lakes 213
July 2004

Preface

I never travel alone when I travel for pleasure. The whole point of it for me is to be able to share, not just the experience and the fun, but also the memories.

And so in these pages you will encounter the many friends and others with whom we have travelled over the years to very many places, and some who have been with us on more than one trip. You will also find the friends we may not have travelled with, but whose presence and friendship in their countries or places we visited were a really important part of our experience there. Through them we were introduced to sights—and sites—we may not have known about; to interesting people we may not otherwise have met; to an understanding and perspective on local political and social events that would have remained elusive. Above all, the warmth and welcome with which they received us made each place special.

Where we go is usually decided spontaneously; one of us might say, 'Let's do a wine trip in France,' or 'We should go to Angkor before it's overrun by tourists,' or simply, over a drink one evening, we may decide we can go to Myanmar now that the generals have announced elections. There are friends we've travelled with more than once who share our sense of fun and finding out about people and places, so then it's just a question of co-ordinating dates. The main thing is—we all love travelling, we all love food, and all of us enjoy each other's company.

Bunny Page (Lake District and Sicicly) is a very old friend, founder-member of the crafts organisation, Dastkar, avid traveller and lover of art and architecture; and her son, Jon, talented photographer and film buff, whom we have known since he was ten. Joanne and Peter Eley, whose house we stayed at in the Lake District, are architects, Pogey's acquaintances. Madhu and Krishna Jain (Bergerac and Dordogne), are old travelling companions, too. Madhu, a senior journalist, earlier with *India Today* for many years, is currently editor of *IQ*, the *India Quarterly*; a film aficionado, art critic and author. Krishna, a physicist at the Indian Institute of Technology (IIT), Delhi, gifted gardener, lover of music, savant. Vishwa is the well-known painter, Vishwanadhan, who lives in Paris, and Nadine, also a painter, is his partner.

Cookie (Saraswathy Ganapathy; Myanmar and Cambodia) is probably our oldest friend, with whom we have travelled often, most memorably on a driving-and-garden trip in south-west Ireland, with Bunny. Raghu is her son, former editor of *TimeOut Delhi*, who was researching Indian soldiers in Burma during World War II at the time, which is why I suspect he accompanied us in the first place! Anna (also Cambodia) is Anna Nadotti, a fine translator of fiction from English into Italian, translator of Anita

Desai, Amitav Ghosh and A.S. Byatt. Anna is the kind of traveller who is not only keenly interested in places and people, but reads up on the country she's travelling to, and so, is wonderfully and intelligently informed about it.

Simone Manceau and Erik Sørensen (Sicily), friends from Paris; Simone translates excellently from English into French, has translated Amit Chaudhuri, Shashi Deshpande, Radhika Jha and Kunal Basu, among others. Erik, retired now from the European Commission, consults on projects for the EU, and they both visit India almost every year.

Rosalba Tana and her daughter and son-in-law, Antonella and Roberto (Sicily), are among our dearest friends, an absolute mine of information on Italy, her museums and art, and are delightful travelling companions. Rosalba lives in Como and is a very good ceramist, painter and weaver; Antonella also weaves, and she and Roberto live outside Rome.

Ayesha Kagal, former print journalist and a producer at NDTV for over twenty years, and her nephew, Vivan, accompanied us in Turkey.

Who else? Oh yes, Pogey and Ratna, my husband and daughter, fellow travellers not only to places far and near, but on life's journey as well.

New Delhi   RITU MENON
June 2016

Myanmar Days

February 2012

It was only in Bagan that I experienced, fully, the serenity of the Buddha. Wandering through the undergrowth around one of the hundreds of pagoda clusters that stud the landscape, I came upon him, his face aglow in the setting sun, the pagoda crumbling, its arches and brickwork jagged, pigeons fluttering in its dim corridors. He wore a smile of such beatitude and there emanated from him such a radiant calm that I, an unbeliever, felt in the presence of divinity.

I was so glad that I had finally seen an unpainted, ungilded, unadorned Buddha in an abandoned temple, surprising because it abutted a complex of restored and landscaped monuments just off the edge of the road. It's true, the whole compound had an air of quietude about it, with no one around, the leaves of its ficus and neem and tamarind trees whispering in the gentle breeze, the many Buddhas in the niches gleaming white, gleaming gold. But it was that solitary figure, pale ochre against the dull red eroding bricks of the pagoda in the sunset, who is imprinted in my mind.

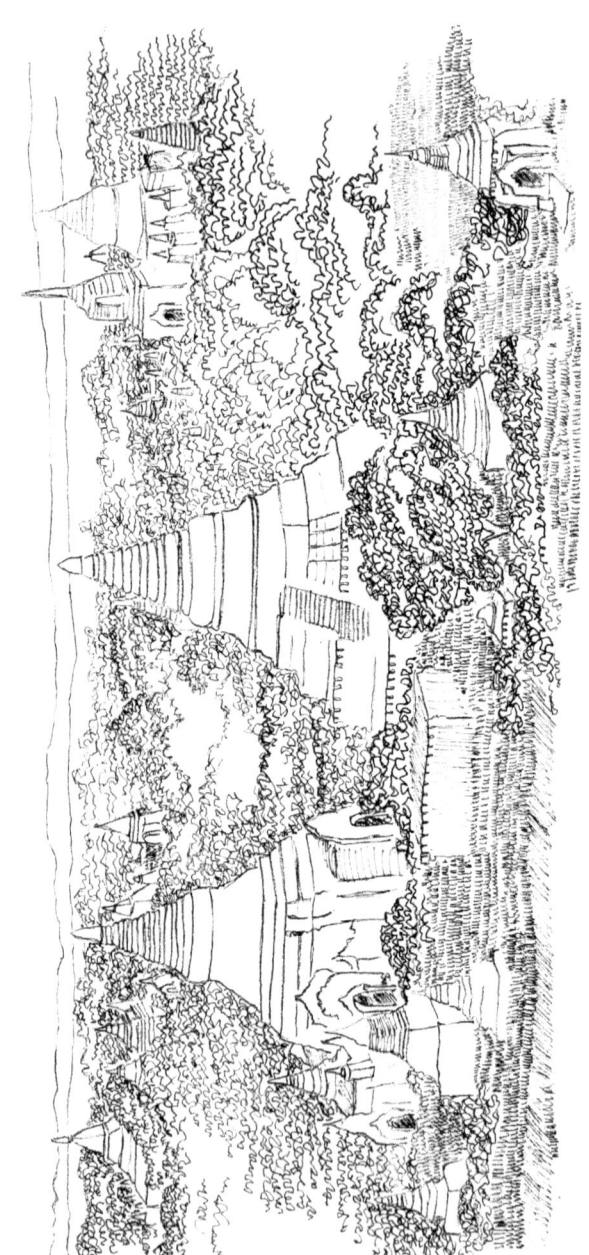

A Profusion of Pagodas in Bagan

It is possible in Old Bagan to let your imagination wander, to pretend you are in the twelfth or thirteenth century when the majority of its approximately 3,000-4,000 temples and stupas were built. The landscape is intermittently jungle and thorny scrub, palm trees with fan-like fronds, neem and tamarind, of course, peepul in all the temple courtyards—and everywhere the terraces and domes and spires of stupas and pagodas emerging from the foliage. As Raghu (Karnad) said, it was as if someone had flung pagoda seeds across the place at random, and pagodas had sprouted and multiplied in breathtaking profusion. Cookie thought that was a lovely image. As far as the eye can see, up to the horizon, in practically every part of Old Bagan, in the distance or on the road, they rise up in veneration and also in a majesty all their own, whether or not any images remain in their sanctum sanctorums. Although all the original eleventh-to thirteenth-century wooden buildings in Bagan have gone, these brick and stucco religious monuments are evidence of the magnificence of the Bagan kings who built feverishly till the Mongol invasions at the end of the thirteenth century. This frenzy of temple-building marked the region's transition from Mahayana to Theravada Buddhism. The Bamar king, Anawrahta, is said to have invaded the kingdom of Manuha, the Mon King of Thatar, and made off with thirty-two sets of the *Tripitaka*, the classic Buddhist scriptures, the city's monks and scholars, and Manuha himself! All because the Mon King had refused to send the texts and relics to Anawrahta when he asked for them.

This marked the beginning of what has been called the First Burmese Empire.

Almost all the pagodas in Bagan are unplastered and ungilded and I hope they remain that way, that they don't become replicas (albeit modest) of Shwedagon in Yangon, that blinds you with its gold. That their precincts remain wooded, the paths to them unpaved, their timelessness preserved. Ironic that the Buddha, whose endeavour his whole life had been to transcend the material world, should be memorialised and worshipped via such materiality.

At Shwedagon in Yangon, this materiality reaches astonishing heights. That profusion in Bagan which was a testament to the power, meritoriousness and glory of those who built and added, here begins to look like unaesthetic excess. Heavily and ornately carved pavilions with garishly painted niches and images, are often lit by twinkling, multicoloured fairy lights, and the Buddha himself sometimes encircled by a halo of on-again, off-again blinking pinpoints of purple, red, green and blue. There are temples for every occasion, dedicated corners for every day of the week, where those born on that day offer up incense, flowers, prayers. It is teeming with devotees, with tourists, with hawkers, with children, teeming and bustling and busily active, so that the material world is all around you and spirituality seems to have made a hasty exit. With such clamour all around, can something as subtle and elusive as the spiritual find refuge?

In the city, it's hard to ignore the march of the material. Old buildings are being torn down rapidly, skyscrapers mushrooming, and ever since Myanmar 'opened up', expatriate Burmese in the US and Thailand and elsewhere are selling their property to cash in on the rising prices of real estate. And not just the expats. Chinese investment stands at 60 per cent of the economy, we were told; Japan is into tourism, travel and trade; the French oil giant, Total, controls 90 per cent of Myanmar's gas and oil reserves; and the Thais are old hands in the timber business. Myanmar-watchers say there has been a 25 per cent surge in the drug trade—several government-cum-private hotels in Yangon, we were told, had been built with drug money. And Chinese–Kachin rivalry over mineral resources in the east, adjoining Yunan province, was escalating. Of the 25 million hectares of teak plantation in the entire Asia–Pacific region, 15 million are in Myanmar; 'If you cut one tree, you are fined 3,000 kyat,' Aung told us, 'but if you cut a whole hectare, it's okay.' Collusion and corruption go hand-in-hand everywhere.

Aung is a tour guide, a very good one, but he is actually a lawyer by training. Born and brought up in Bagan, he studied law in Mandalay; he practised for a year then gave up. Too much corruption, he said, not enough civil law, and—in an unwitting give-away—'very little crimes'. He's been a guide for six years now, supporting his two younger siblings at university in Mandalay, but hopes to return to lawyering now that democracy seems to be in the offing. One week ago he applied for membership to Aung San Suu Kyi's National League for Democracy (NLD), and was part of the Bagan unit's reception committee when she came campaigning to the area. Might he enter politics? we asked. He nodded, then added, 'That's why I study law—lawyers are liars, good in politics.' Not many young men and women are politically inclined, he said, not even among his friends, but he participated in 2007's Saffron Demonstration; although he wasn't arrested he was certainly interrogated, so somewhere in the data banks of the junta, his name must already be recorded. Wasn't he taking a risk, we asked, surely it was still dangerous to be politically active? He shrugged and laughed his easy laugh. 'No pain, no gain,' he chortled, 'but my parents, yes, they don't like it. They worry.'

Although the generals and President U Thein Sein have relaxed censorship, freed several thousand political prisoners, legalised the NLD and trade unions, people are still very careful. Fifty years of living behind the Bamboo Curtain have ingrained habits of caution, and real news is hard to come by. The government has indeed signed a ceasefire agreement with the Karen, Myanmar's largest minority tribe, but the Kachin continue to be recalcitrant; and General Aung San's Museum officially opens only on one day in the year—19 July, the date on which he was assassinated in 1947. No one knows why.

Nay Pyi Taw, the new capital, is 300 km away from Yangon, with no airport—accessible only by road; and on 10 February, the day we left Myanmar, we heard that a senior monk who was released in 2011, had been re-arrested.

* * *

U Sein Maung is a musician and music teacher, and his family of musicians plays at all novitiation ceremonies and festive occasions in the village adjoining our hotel in Old Bagan. The village consists of about seventy families, living in thatch and bamboo houses on stilts at the edge of the Irrawaddy. It is the cleanest village I have ever seen. Mud roads, swept clean of rubbish, leaves, scraps, litter; cattle in the compounds, homestead farming in the riverbeds and flats. Its primary school has seventy-five students taught by six teachers in rotation. Myanmar spends 4 per cent of its GDP on education; the demand now is that this be raised to 10 per cent (defence expenditure is at 15 per cent). A young mother we spoke to said all deliveries and births now take place in hospitals, but that they had to pay up to USD 120 as a bribe in order to be served. 'Corruption!' exclaimed Aung, 'if you don't pay you don't get medical care.' Surely schooling is free, though? 'Yes,' he said, 'but not books or uniforms' (these are green longyis and white or coloured tops for all boys and girls across the country).

U Sein Maung's four children are adopted and they all play a musical instrument or instruments. He is a master drummer and xylophonist, as is his young son; his daughter sings and accompanies on the cymbals; and the youngest boy is learning to drum. It was the sound of U Sein tuning his drums that led us to his house—a handsome wood and bamboo structure with a music room on the upper floor, where he sat in a circular enclosure with about ten drums of different sizes and pitches surrounding him. As he applied a resin-like substance on the drum he spat on it, smoothed and evened it out, then struck it, to test its pitch. After he had tuned each one, he and his children treated us to one of the most musical and enjoyable impromptu performances we had ever heard. We couldn't tell if it was popular or folk, but it had the rhythm and percussive quality of jazz—certainly not what you would expect to hear in a dusty Myanmar village!

Aung promised to show us a sunset in Bagan at a pagoda that wasn't swarming with people. We drove past the Shwesandaw—whose terraces were dotted with people and where, just the day before, we had spent a wonderful morning with not another soul in sight—then took a sharp right down a dirt track. Nestled between keekar-like trees was a little jewel of a temple. It glowed pink in the dying light, was as quiet as a grave, had not a single Buddha image in it, and from its uppermost terrace we watched as the sun sank slowly over the horizon; the stupas and temples around us and in the near distance were first lit by gold, then darkened abruptly as the sun dropped out of sight. In the afterglow which lingered for several minutes, the silhouetted spires and domes vied for space with the trees, and with each other, in the twilight sky.

The splendour of the pagodas in Bagan lies in their sheer number and in their clustering, but also undoubtedly in the fact that there are no habitations in the vicinity of the archaeological environment. All the villages in the area were relocated to New Bagan in the early 1990s, within a period of three months. Aung showed us where his home had been before they were shunted out. 'No compensation,' he said, 'only land.' Heritage over Humans has always been a vexed issue, to which no satisfactory resolution seems to have been found in our part of the world.

The next morning at sunrise, as a pink smudge spread across the sky, the pagoda spires were picked out by deep pink highlights that diffused into a rose glow as the sky lightened and the day dawned. Like a scattering of rubies against a jade green backdrop.

For the rest, and speaking for myself, one pagoda is much like another with the obvious exception of a few. Shwesandaw, the first temple we visited (built to commemorate the conquest of Thaton) afforded spectacular views and a breathtaking vista of spires and domes; and Sula-man-i, Aung's favourite twelfth-century pagoda, had some lovely murals and exquisite tile plaques with scenes from the *Jataka* on the exterior walls. It also had the distinction of having been used as a hospital by the British during the World War II—a use its 100 underground monks' cells could hardly have anticipated. Ananda Paya is certainly the most splendid with its 170-ft high shimmering spire; also the most venerated temple in Bagan, but the Shwezigon, although not as over-the-top as Shwedagon, is still much too gilded for my liking.

* * *

We met Nang Pyore May, a local villager, the day we arrived in Inle. May's maternal grandfather came down from the mountains in Shan state to Nyaungshwe, the gateway village for Inle Lake. A farmer, he also tapped the lac tree for resin which he sold to boat-makers on the lake. When he came down to the valley he opened a small goods shop, and May grew up partly on the lake and partly in Nyaungshwe. Strewn along the lake, and sometimes in the middle of it, are a series of water villages, built almost entirely on stilts, in bamboo and thatch again, and all traffic is by boat alone. So is all farming. The lake is criss-crossed with floating gardens where the Intha (as the local inhabitants are called) grow tomatoes, cucumbers, pumpkins, garlic and onions, tending their plants, turning the soil, fertilising and anchoring it—all from their boats. Those postcard photographs of bamboo poles angling up from the water, silhouetted against a painted sunset, are from lakes like Inle, where the poles are sunk into the water to fence in the gardens and keep them from shifting too far. It's an ingenious device and it must require considerable skill to farm in this way, but it's nowhere near the sheer virtuosity displayed by the fishermen—often mere striplings—as they paddle with one leg, throw their nets and manoeuvre their boats, while thrashing the water to chase the fish into the nets, all at the same time! In one seamless coordinated movement. A water ballet. The nets themselves are shaped like cones that collapse and fan out, held in tension by a delicate tracery of what must be a bamboo frame, glistening in the sunlight. Intha children, May told us, learn to swim almost before they learn to walk, and they are taught to work the oars soon after. Men fish and farm and women weave and roll cheroots; to see thread being drawn out of lotus stems in a deft, nimble operation is to be struck by the ingenuity of the woman who, about sixty years ago, first experimented with the stem. It's now a thriving skill and industry, yielding a soft, rich, supple yarn which, either by itself or teamed up with silk, is fashioned into scarves, shirts and other garments. Intricate ikat weaving in silk and cotton, also common, is a reminder that this craft stretches all the way from Central Asia to Japan, with Chinese lookalikes now flooding markets in South-east Asia. On the Inle looms, however, ikat is woven primarily by women, unlike in India where it is a male-dominated craft.

It's apparent that the Intha have lived like this for years, and were it not for the occasional signboard announcing computer classes in the midst of homes and schools, you could be excused for thinking that life will continue like this in the foreseeable future. The lake is large enough—13.5 miles long and seven miles wide—and the villages and population dispersed enough for their lifestyle and livelihoods to remain sustainable for a good long while, because immigration into the area is now disallowed. But tourism has extended its tentacles into the area and it's sure to disturb the delicate balance between humans and nature that prevails. One can only hope that the people's spontaneous, completely genuine hospitality and gentle manner of interacting remain intact.

Half a century of near-isolation has had unhappy consequences; the country has seen brutal repression and censorship and faced economic sanctions, all of which make for an uneasy response to a first encounter with Myanmar.

Aung San Suu Kyi's famous gate addresses now take place behind a high wall around her house, no longer visible from University Avenue. You're never sure who owns what, whether it's the government, the military, or its cronies, so all spending may be lining some undesirable pockets. All tourist travel is recorded—Myanmar is probably the only country in the world where each time you fly within the country, you have to pass through 'immigration'. Surveillance of one sort or another almost certainly takes place, and because books and periodicals from outside were more or less totally proscribed, Yangon's 'open air libraries', the second-hand pavement bookshops, are full of pre-1950s literature. War memoirs, pirated copies of George Orwell's *Burma Days*, Rudyard Kipling, naturally, and *The Road to Mandalay*.

But how refreshing to be in a country that hasn't yet been penetrated by globalisation, where cities are free of high-rises and flyovers, where roads are safe, and crime negligible. Where ordinary people are unaggressive and helpful; where the air is clean and you can still see stars in the sky.

Cambodia: The Buddhas of Bayon

January 2005

It's hard to know where to begin this account of our trip to Cambodia—with our arrival in Siem Riep on the 21st morning, having met Cookie at Bangkok airport? Or with our arrival at the utterly charming Hotel Borann, bungalows around a lush tropical garden, four rooms to each bungalow? Beautifully furnished, cool and comfortable. With our impromptu lunch at Jacques Gaucher's house, down the road from the hotel? Or with our very unexpected, rather strenuous hike up a steep, rocky hill to see the sun set over Angkor Wat, from Phnom Bakeng?

We were five—Anna from Turin; Cookie from Bangalore; Pogey, Ratna and me.

I think I'll begin with the Bayon, the magnificent Buddhist temple built in the 1200s by the Khmer kings, Jayavarman VII and VIII, about 200 years after Angkor Wat. The Bayon is in the city of Angkor Thom, to the north of Angkor Wat. Jacques, Pogey's friend and colleague from Paris, has been in Cambodia for ten years, studying Angkor Thom intensively for the last four. At lunch in his home the

The Buddhas of Bayon

day we arrived, he gave us a synoptic view of Khmer temple architecture and the hundreds of temples that dot the country, as well as of some aspects—a very few, he would say—of Khmer culture. Although we were sleepy and not nearly as attentive as we should have been, his account of what Cambodia had been through during the last thirty years, and of what this has meant for Khmer society today, was a very good introduction. Nothing he told us about Angkor Thom that day, however, prepared us for the Bayon, the last of Jayavarman VII's great mountain temples, built in the late twelfth and early thirteenth centuries.

One usually visits the Bayon after Angkor Wat, this being the chronological order in which the temples were constructed, but we did the opposite. I think we were right. So we set off early—every morning at 8 o'clock for the whole week—in our tuk-tuks (same term as in Bangladesh) and drove along the moat that surrounds Angkor Wat, past Phnom Bakeng, whose hillside we had toiled up the previous evening (not a soul to be seen there now—everyone goes there at sunset because that's what the guidebooks recommend), then north to the city of Angkor Thom. Poor Cookie had to stay back because she had a sore eye. (And by the end of the trip, Ratna had a very sore throat.) A marvellous tree-lined, shady drive to the Bayon at the easy, breezy pace of the tuk-tuk and you relax in your seat, enjoying the balmy air. Then suddenly, without warning, you see the south gate of the temple with its four massive heads of—Jayavarman? The Buddha as Lokisvara, lord of the four corners of the world? It's an open question still. No matter, the sight is staggering. Then as you get closer, there's about 100 metres of the approach road with a row of asuras and gods on either side, sculpted to show Manthan, the Churning of the Ocean of Milk. At Angkor Wat, the bas reliefs show eighty-eight demons and ninety-two gods; there aren't that many here but the sight is absolutely stunning—and it does evoke a sense of heightened anticipation.

The temple itself hits you between the eyes. One hundred and seventy-one massive heads, impassive and enigmatic, or enigmatically smiling, look down on you from every corner of the temple. Its three or four levels are staggered, mimicking the ascent to Mount Meru, Shiva's abode (hence, mountain temples), and the heads adorn the several gopurams at each level. They look down, or across, or askance from each level simultaneously, following devotees with their all-seeing gaze. The immensity of the temple and the faces are what remain of the Bayon experience for me. Even though there were hordes of noisy Japanese intent only on getting themselves photographed—did they actually see anything, we wondered—and some rather wonderful bas reliefs on the eastern wall, it's the sheer drama of the space, the banked levels, enclosures surrounded by just those huge faces, that are an indelible imprint.

The overlay of Buddhist on Hindu is a most unusual characteristic of the temples at Angkor. So the Bayon is a three-dimensional rendering of the cosmic manthan, the battle between good and evil, but it is also Buddhist. The transition from the dominance of one religion—Hinduism in this case—to another (Buddhism) can sometimes take hundreds of years, during which period a most interesting co-existence is possible, and you see this clearly in Angkorian temples.

About the only traveller's account that there is of Angkor Thom, Jacques told us, is by a thirteenth-century Chinese who reported that the faces of the Bayon were covered with gold leaf, and that the 'glittering towers of Angkor Thom' could be seen from afar. What a magnificent sight it must have been!

We left the Bayon to meet Jacques at Angkor Wat for an early lunch at Matthieu and Sophea's restaurant across the road from the temple. Matthieu is French, married to Sophea, a Cambodian, and a dancer. Much younger than him, we thought. They had cooked a Khmer–French meal for us which, culinarily speaking, was as splendid as the Bayon. Dried beef to begin with, followed by perfectly fried fish accompanied by a deliciously tart sauce; followed in turn by chicken in a light, delicately flavoured banana flower sauce, absolutely scrumptious; coupled with salad, green and crisp, a light rosé, and warm, flaky baguettes. We could hardly keep from exclaiming after every mouthful, it was all so delectable. Then, when we were so full that we could hardly move, Matthieu (quite a raconteur himself) produced dragon-fruit and mango steeped in Cointreau. And here we were, planning to see Angkor Wat through an alcoholic haze! The situation was retrieved somewhat by Matthieu's excellent coffee (the only good coffee we had during the whole trip), after which we said a prolonged goodbye, promised to return (which we did), P and R went back to the hotel to fetch Cookie, and Anna and I made our way to Angkor Wat.

The thing about these Angkor temples is that they are so grand in their conception, there's nothing ordinary or modest about them. You have to walk and walk and climb and climb to reach the abode of the gods; they have moats around them, many of them, long causeways supposedly separating, or marking, the transition from the world of men to the world of gods, and concentric galleries and gopurams that symbolically represent Mount Meru. To reach the sanctum sanctorum you have to climb to the highest level, often up very steep and narrow steps. Angkor Wat, almost completely restored now, is one of the finest examples of this type of temple and the largest Hindu temple in the world. In fact, the whole concept of a mountain temple is unique to the Khmer—there are none in India.

There's no way one can imagine the grandeur and sophistication of Angkor Wat, and I honestly don't think I can describe it adequately. Its magisterial scale and confident execution, the beauty and fineness of its bas reliefs, the level of craftsmanship, and the sheer magnitude of the endeavour—it's phenomenal. Wall after wall, metres and metres of the legend of the *Mahabharata*, the churning of the ocean of milk, scenes from daily life, triumphal processions…apsaras and asuras, kings and commoners, crocodiles and fish and turtles and parrots and the most exquisitely carved foliage. It was absolutely astounding. And, really, it has to be seen to be believed.

By the time we left the temple, our muscles were screaming and joints creaking, and we were footsore but happily sated. We returned gratefully to the hotel for a shower, and then to Jacques' place because he was going to show us the work he has been doing on Angkor Thom.

Jacques believes that Angkor Thom is actually a far more important site than Angkor Wat because it is a whole city, conceived, visualised and laid out in a complex grid of streets, water channels, ponds and residential areas that suggest a sophisticated urban sensibility. In other words, it wasn't all temples. Jacques' four years of systematically uncovering layer upon layer of the materiality of Angkor Thom is truly remarkable, and as he explicated his methodology, accompanied by photographs, diagrams, computer-generated maps and grids of amazing detail, it was like seeing an archaeological-cum-architectural thriller unfolding. In Pogey's reckoning, if his hypothesis is accepted and he has the evidence to back it up, it will be a major contribution to the study of Angkoriana. At any rate, we were completely riveted by his exposition.

Still discussing and talking, we left Jacques' place at 10 p.m. and looked for a restaurant where we could eat, but it was late and most places were closed. Finally, we walked along the river that runs through Siem Reap (in the middle of the town, quite charming) to the Victoria Hotel built in the French–Vietnamese style. Very pleasing environment, but the food was unremarkable. By this time we were ready for bed, completely and utterly satisfied.

Waking up at the Borann was a lovely experience. You walked out into the garden full of hibiscus and birds of paradise and assorted palms and birdsong. Tea in bed, shower and change, and out by 8 or 8.15 a.m. Cookie complaining loudly about early starts, Anna complaining politely that it was already late! Jacques was going to take us to Banteay Srei, an early and the only, sandstone temple in Angkor, via another site, the Kbal Spean, a river in the forest which has riverbed sculptures, dating to the eleventh–twelfth centuries.

Before that, though, Jacques said he wanted to show us the Western Baray, a huge 8 km x 2.5 km reservoir built by Suryavarman I in the eleventh century, which is still a most impressive sight. Even more impressive, almost unbelievable, is the fact that it covers an area of 1,760 hectares and was *excavated entirely by hand*. No wonder, then, that all these monumental works were serviced by tens of thousands of servants. On the way Jacques told us how, when he began working in the area, they had to cut through the jungle with a machete, look out for landmines—which were laid almost next to each other all along the border with Vietnam, but also infested the Angkor area—and all manner of poisonous snakes. The first time he went to Angkor Thom, he said, they were accompanied by six soldiers with guns!

We didn't realise quite how far Kbal Spean was from Banteay Srei. About 16 km on a very rough country road. Poor P and R, sitting on the flatbed of a Toyota pick-up van, would have been most uncomfortable. We heaved a sigh of relief when we reached, but worse was to come—a one-hour trek, on quite difficult terrain, uphill, to the riverbed carvings. Cookie gave up about halfway, I soldiered on, following Jacques, P and R and Anna. Towards the end, though, I got a bit lost as the trails forked and the others were nowhere in sight. Panicking a bit (it's no fun being alone in a jungle, even in the middle of the day) I stumbled upon the riverbed sculptures by accident—Vishnu reclining, Shiva and the bull, assorted others, quite unusual—but was too disoriented to take them in. Finally, Ratna spotted me and we were together again, but I was rather cross at having been thus abandoned.

After lunch at one of the local stalls—clusters of little children surround you at all these sites selling their wares. 'Madaam, you buy ten postcards for one dollaa…madaam, one guide book, five dollaa, madaam, you want water? cold drink?'—as we retraced our way to Banteay Srei.

Which is truly special. A small temple, almost miniature by Angkor standards, but intricately carved bas reliefs of uncommon depth. Unfortunately, the best part of the temple was closed for restoration but we did have a good look from the outside, and it's small enough to give some idea of the whole. Jacques thinks that this was a one-off temple, probably carved by Indian artisans, because there's nothing else like it before or since. Nothing extant, that is.

From here we went to Pre Rup (96 AD), generally assumed to be a funerary temple—again, unusual in Hinduism—and then to Ta Keo, begun by Jayavarman V, but left unfinished. But by this time, Cookie and I were exhausted and decided to leave the others and return to the hotel. A refreshing cup of tea and we headed off for a spot of retail therapy! Well deserved in my case, said Cookie, but not in hers.

Got back, met the others for a drink, had a pedestrian dinner at the Borann and fell into bed to sleep the sleep of the dead.

The next day we saw the restoration work at Baphuon, the highest of the Angkor temples, north-east of the Bayon in Angkor Thom. Jacques had asked his friend and former student, Pascal, in charge of the restoration, to show us around and explain the work they were doing. Like all the other temples, Baphuon, too, was in an advanced state of destruction when the French began restoring it in the 1960s and 1970s. In the early 1970s, they were forced to abruptly abandon work because Angkor was taken over by the Khmer Rouge. The entire archive of the project was destroyed by the Khmer—documents, drawings, an inventory of objects, photographs and maps. When the site was opened up again in 1995, the French had to start from scratch, but without the benefit of any of the previous records. So, not just the restoration of the monument, but a reconstruction of their own work, as well.

As we walked through the temple, up steps and scaffolding, Jacques and Pascal explained the basis of the restoration decisions they had taken, the debates on how much, and how, to restore—should it be restored to its original eleventh-century form or include the later, sixteenth-century, Buddhist elements as well? Part of the temple had been destroyed to accommodate a massive reclining Buddha—which Pascal quaintly kept referring to as the Retaining Buddha, so preoccupied was he with retaining walls on the monument! The Buddha was never completed, it's only a rough image carved in stone. The Cambodians didn't want him there at all and preferred to restore the temple to its original eleventh-century glory, but the ultimate decision was to stick to the sixteenth-century elements, the last recorded additions. The question of whose history should be restored is clearly political, and as Jacques said, a political choice had to be made.

We were all struck again by Pascal and Jacques' deep knowledge of the temples and of Angkor history and architecture, and their passionate involvement with its culture. Jacques was full of information and insights into archaeology and architecture, but also transparently humanistic in his approach to his work. Such a privilege to have had him with us as friend, philosopher and guide—it completely transformed our experience of Angkor, made it memorable and very special.

From Baphuon we walked across to the Royal Palace, where Jacques had carried out his first excavations to establish the antiquity of the city. He told us that they had found evidence of building up to five metres below the ground, indicating several layers of built history, going back at least five centuries before the current extant structures. Fascinating, the detail with which he recounted the building of the palace just adjoining the temple of Phimeanakas, built earlier, the laying of the tank alongside, elaborately carved along its embankments, and the Elephant Terrace along the outside boundary wall on the east. A terrace of wonderfully playful and realistically carved elephants, still very well preserved. And, across the road—which was previously the river—a series of small temples which had been sited on the river's opposite bank, across from the palace. Pogey was struck by the brilliance of that imagination which had visualised the vista so dramatically. As he said, no Hindu city or temple in India had ever been conceptualised on this scale, so that as an ensemble, Angkor is *sui generis*. Jacques wondered if it may not have been a Utopia realised.

We left them then and made our way to Ta Prohm, a temple built by Jayavarman VII to venerate his mother, and now almost completely overrun by the jungle. What an extraordinary builder he was, responsible for the Bayon, Ta Prohm, the Western Baray and a host of smaller prasats and temples.

Ta Prohm is enough to give you just a hint of what Angkor Wat and all the other temples must have looked like when Henri Mouhot stumbled upon them in 1863. Buried under a tangle of trees whose roots and trunks and branches devoured the stones of the monuments, dark and impenetrable. Ta Prohm has been partially cleared, enough to let you walk through it, but enough has also been left as is, the inexorable passage of time a palpable and intensely humbling realisation. Of course, we had seen photographs of the temple with trees growing out of the Buddha's eyes on the south gate, crushing the magnificent structure under their weight, but walking through the rubble of this ruin is an experience of a different order.

Three centuries of silk-cotton and fig trees soar up to the sky, their enormous roots curling and twisting and snaking along lintels and doors and openings, ripping open its innards, casually destroying its composition. Through the debris of stones and fallen carvings, you glimpse an apsara or two, a goddess here and there, perfectly preserved, a slow smile on her face, hands held in a graceful mudra. Around her, the collapse of a dynasty, almost of a civilisation, the sharp cry of a parrot as it streaks past overhead, the stillness of an abandoned courtyard.

The temple compound is enormous, 1 km by 650 mt, and as you walk through it from east to west, you begin to understand why it is important to leave it more or less as it is, why it shouldn't be cleaned up and restored like Angkor Wat. Somewhere, evidence of the impermanence of things must be allowed to remain. A thousand years separate us from the kings who built Angkor, and those thousand years are almost tangible at Ta Prohm. You can feel their passing, almost hear the cracking and splitting of stone, the crumbling of an edifice to God.

All is vanity.

In the evening, Anna, Ratna and I decided to see the Bayon by moonlight, a farewell to the great temple before leaving the next morning. Our tuk-tuk driver, Ra, thought we were mad but drove us there nevertheless, on streets now quite deserted. Dusk was falling, and as we neared the south gate, the moon cast a pale light through the trees on the asuras on either side of the road. By the time we reached the temple, the light was silvery and the entire landscape, hushed. The huge structure loomed formidably in the distance, and we were glad that there were at least three of us together. In any case, we were the only ones there. We walked up the causeway at the east gate, through the first gopuram and out into the courtyard from where we could see the massive heads of the central courtyard, half in shadow, half in moonlight, silhouetted against the deepening sky. It was mesmerising. I don't know how long I stood there, gazing at this surreal sight, before realising that Anna and Ratna had vanished up the dark steps to the central courtyard. Very risky, really, because night was falling rapidly and the stairwell would be pitch-dark in no time. I called to them to come down quickly and started moving out myself, when suddenly the whole northern section of the temple was ablaze with light. For a full five minutes those giant heads were lit up, dazzling us with their majesty. You can imagine what a spectacular moment it was. We gasped in disbelief. Who had switched on those lights, and why? Were they motion sensors, activated by Ratna and Anna's presence? Were they timed? Who knows. All I know is that it is that last vision of the Bayon that has imprinted itself on my mind's eye, an unforgettable sight.

That evening, our last in Siem Riep, Jacques invited all of us and Pascal to dinner at Madame Butterfly's, a restaurant serving the most delicious Khmer food, and a favourite haunt of the French ministry of culture on their trips to Angkor. We had a huge seven-course meal, much,

much more than we could possibly eat, but the eating was interspersed with wine and conversation that flowed and ebbed as we ate. Jacques grew more and more nostalgic as he reminisced about his time in South-east Asia, and especially about Vietnam. Vietnam, he said, was an affair of the heart for the French, Cambodia was a matter for the head. He can't bear to return to Vietnam, he said, he's almost on the verge of tears all the time that he's there. He was so transparent in his affection, so sincere, that we didn't have the heart to question him. But it did trigger off a discussion on colonialism, French versus English, the experience of India and Africa, and so on. Of course, Jacques has spent years in Tamil Nadu and Chandernagore, so he knows the difference. But Pascal had had a quite different experience of Cambodia and so the conversation between him and Jacques was most interesting.

A long while later we left the restaurant, said a very sad goodbye to Jacques and Pascal, and returned to the hotel. We were really sorry to be leaving the next morning—sorry to leave Angkor, sorrier still to be leaving Jacques....

The next day, 25 January, on the long, long boat ride to Phnom Penh, down the Tonle Sap—the largest lake in South-east Asia—and later, the Mekong, we had more than enough time to absorb and think about everything we had seen and heard. Out on the lake and river we saw something of the limpid countryside that is almost symbolic of South-east Asia—fishing villages, gentle vegetation, an unending horizon with palm trees in the far distance. But also desperate poverty. This is a country that has been traumatised by more than thirty years of violence and decimation. A whole generation wiped out, the economy devastated, social and cultural distress on a frightening scale. And now—tourism, tourism, tourism. Is this the only antidote the world has to offer Cambodia? It's there in a big way, the world, pouring millions and millions of dollars into restoring Angkor. Which it should—but there's no money for education or health or any other kind of development. The children go a-begging, or are horribly exploited. The first thing that greets you at the airport is public service advertisements against child sexual abuse—the extent of trafficking to Thailand and Vietnam is quite alarming. Surely tourism can't alleviate all this? Just couldn't help coming back to the cruel juxtaposition of life and art, again and again, throughout this trip.

Borobodur and Bali: 'Maybe Later?'

July 2007

The Ministry of Coffee is an unusual name for a hotel, but then this was a somewhat unusual place for the street we were on in Yogyakarta. Prawirotaman is in old Yogya, but it's sort of shabby and rundown, the equivalent of Paharganj, according to Pogey, full of mid-range tourist accommodation, mostly unremarkable. But the Ministry of Coffee is light, airy, very gracious in its hospitality—and, as the book says, has the best cakes, pastries and coffee in Yogya. Not surprisingly, it's been set up to promote Javanese coffee, and it seems to be succeeding. (Now I know why the coffee hangout in Bangalore is called Java City.)

But our room was tiny! Barely enough room to move, one of those showers that you need a shoehorn to get into, and a cupboard with barely enough space for a few hangers. However, the staff couldn't have been more charming, and anyway, all we did in the room was sleep. (Ubud couldn't have been more of a contrast, but more of that later.) Not being able to unpack our things, we simply set our bags down and went out to explore the town.

Walking was difficult, because we were in imminent

With Rana at Rio Helmi's House in Bali

danger of being mowed down by motor-cyclists—*everyone* in Yogya seems to roar past on motorbikes—there were no sidewalks to speak of, and the streets were fairly dirty and potholed. Still. Wandered into a couple of antique shops, bought a few essentials at a local department store, and made our way back to the Ministry.

Prawirotaman, and it seemed much of Yogya, is made up of small shops, petty businesses, dozens of automobile spare parts and motorbike showrooms—and scores of shopfronts with small goods. Assorted household items, groceries and provisions, clothes, bric-a-brac, money-changers, tour operators, Internet kiosks, batik shops, the ubiquitous travel agents selling Borobudur, Prambanam, Surabaya, Denpasar, and all the other popular tourist destinations. Everyone is unfailingly courteous, even the touts are polite and helpful (unlike in India where they are aggressive and overbearing), so you don't mind being accosted by *becak* drivers every few yards, who when you decline, ask hopefully, 'Maybe later?' 'Maybe later' became like a kind of signature, a way of saying there's hope yet for a possible deal.

We decided we'd take a taxi to Borobudur the next day, stop at the temple of Prambanam on the way back, and make a day of it. And, having made the booking, returned to our little lair, showered and changed, and set out to have what I think was the best Indonesian meal we have ever had, at Warung Opera. Funny name for a restaurant or resto, as the Indonesians say, charmingly! Warung Opera was badly damaged in the earthquake of 2006, which hit

Yogya with a reading of 5.8 on the Richter scale. Donny, the owner (a Catholic in predominantly Muslim Yogya) rebuilt it and is back in business with food he cooks himself, from what he grows himself—mostly.

We were the only ones there. Always a bit disconcerting for tourists because you begin to doubt your choice. But the place was totally charming, full of old family furniture, we were surrounded by frangipani and helenconia and palms of all varieties, and made to feel specially welcome. Donny himself chose our dishes for us—and it was a truly delicious meal. Fresh, delicately flavoured, and made only for us. The best Nasi Goreng I have eaten, succulent and tender fresh prawns, lotus flower and tomato sambol. Superb. Why did he call his 'warung'—meaning, variously, shop/business/restaurant—'Opera'? 'Because I sing it,' he replied guilelessly, 'and I like it.' Simple, really. Donny sat and chatted with us throughout, about being Catholic, being separated, being a restauranteur in Indonesia today.

It is after all, the world's largest Muslim country. In Yogya, we were reminded of this five times a day with the musical muezzin, which I love, but also because so many, so very many, young women (including those at our hotel) are covered from head to toe in the hijab.

In Paris, our Indonesian friend Kunang had mentioned that it is not possible to have an interfaith marriage in Indonesia—you have to convert. There is no secular civil law that legitimises a marriage between Muslims and non-Muslims. Her own husband, Michel, a French Catholic, had converted to Islam in order to marry her. And indeed,

I recalled that our Dutch author Saskia (Wieringa) too, had converted to 'marry' her Indonesian partner.

How almost incredible this seems. Indonesia has been dominantly Hindu, then dominantly Hindu–Buddhist, Buddhist, and now Muslim. All three survive in Hindu Bali, Muslim Java and Sumatra, and hybrid Borneo. Yet Kunang's sister, Rana, in Bali, worries about Indonesia becoming a theocratic state. There'll be no place for her then, Muslim by birth, Buddhist by conviction, living in Hindu Bali. None of this seemed to worry Erize and the other young women at the Ministry of Coffee as they went about their business, fully covered, but in the company of men at work. Because we saw scores of women whose heads were not covered, we thought perhaps these ones came from orthodox families. But they were working outside the home… Did covering themselves assure greater mobility? Perhaps. Some things are counter-intuitive, as we know.

We set off for Borobudur after Pogey had his (delicious) breakfast of pancakes and I had some fruit, which was nowhere near as good as the fruit in Bangkok or Sri Lanka. Coffee was divine, though. Heading out north-west of Yogya we drove through the city, past the Sultan's Palace, and saw a more prosperous but still modest, part of Yogya. Roads seemed to be endlessly lined with small shops, residential areas hidden behind them, perhaps? We had seen very few houses so far.

An hour's drive brought us to the great stupa of Borobudur, a monument we had always wanted to see, along with Angkor, and Bagan in Myanmar.

As with Angkor Wat—and Ellora and Konarak and Khajuraho and Notre Dame and all other monumental and magnificent places of worship—the sheer scale of the buildings is staggering. With Borobudur, the siting is also dramatic, with the stupa sitting atop a hill which rises from a flat plain; you see just its silhouette initially, imagining the rest, the seven levels rising up to the concentric circles of stupas, and then the crowning stupa, the culmination of your journey—in life, on earth—in nirvana. The stupa you cannot enter.

Borobudur was built over a hundred years, from AD 750–850 by the Sailendras. A massive amount of stone, about 60,000 cubic metres of it, would have been hewn, transported and carved on site. It's thought that Borobudur is a derivative of the Sanskrit Vihara Buddha Uhr, meaning Buddhist Monastery on a Hill.

It's survived weathering, volcanic eruptions, bombings. Indeed, its survival could be a result of having been buried under volcanic ash for hundreds of years. In 1815, Sir Stamford Raffles, as governor of Java, had the site cleared up, revealing the most stupendous structure. Restoration was begun by the Dutch in the early twentieth century, but over the years the hill had become waterlogged and the immense stone mass began to subside. Between 1973 and 1983 a huge amount of money, USD 25 million, was spent on a mammoth restoration job.

It's truly a sight to behold. And, it seems, to bomb. In 1985, President Soeharto's opponents planted bombs on the upper levels which exploded and damaged some stupas.

They have since been restored, but the site itself seems curiously vulnerable. A relatively easy target.

The day was warm, the sun high in the sky as we began our climb up to the stupas. The lower levels bore carved scenes of everyday life, stages in the stories of the Buddha's enlightenment—but carved and assembled, rather than being carved out of the rock-face. Again, as in India and Cambodia, the carvings are at once delicate and sophisticated. An imagination that could conceive something so monumental, yet subtle, is truly remarkable. As you climb higher, statues of the serene Buddha on all four sides replace the carvings of men and animals, and one is confronted again by the enigma of belief—its strength and its power. Never having been believers, we are struck again and again by its staying power, by the splendour of its creations in brick and stone and marble.

Four levels of terraces, and then three concentric circles of stupas, atop which is the last, large majestic one. The ritual of circumambulation rekindles the magic of the circle itself; the rhythm of the stupas and Buddha faces is mesmerising: whichever way you turn, you see them and are 'seen' by them. The whole is supposed to represent a Buddhist–Tantric mandala, and indeed it is believed that the people who once supported Borobudur were early Vajrayana or Tantric Buddhists who used it as a walk-through mandala.

And yet, and yet. The power and glory of the Bayon in Angkor Thom, it seems to me, far outstrip Borobudur. Is it the Buddhas themselves, more massive yet elusive at the Bayon? Could it be the environment, jungle and overgrown foliage, as distinct from flat plain? Or is it that Angkor has so much more, so very many temples, so many extraordinary built structures, such impressive barais that you have a sense of the civilisation, and their combined impact is far greater?

I don't know. In Ubud, later, we saw one of Rio Helmi's (Kunang's brother) photographs of Borobudur taken very, very early in the morning. Almost pre-dawn. Pale lilac, the monument hovers in the background, almost weightless, ethereal, looking for all the world like the feathery palm fronds and foliage in the foreground. Completely one with the landscape.

Post-lunch at a small wayside resto in the vicinity, we set off for Prambanam, due east. In the opposite direction from Borobudur, so we passed Yogya again, and an hour later were at Prambanam. But what a disappointment! We had thought we would see the two major sites of Indonesia, Buddhist Borobudur and Hindu Prambanam, but Prambanam was cordoned off. The earthquake of 2006 had damaged parts of the monument, so entry was severely restricted. All we could do was walk around the nine temples in the complex that is extant. It must have been an impressive ensemble when all the temples were intact, but now all we could see was the one complex of nine, and ruins of the others scattered across the 'tourist park'. Even the nine are not terribly impressive, except for the fact that they display the union of Hindu–Buddhist elements, there having been a royal marriage that sealed the union. So there are stupa-like structures on the temples, and a stupa rather than a shikhara on top, but other than that…

After this, the lemon and cheese cake—the best I have ever had anywhere—at the Ministry of Coffee was very welcome, not at all disappointing, and a most satisfying coda to our day. We decided to eat at the hotel itself, on the terrace, and call it a day.

The next day we saw something of the city, beginning with the Sultan's Palace. Climbed onto a *becak* outside our hotel, and rode through parts of Yogya that we suspected must exist but hadn't yet seen. All parts of the palace compound, a walled enclosure of several kilometres which houses more than 25,000 people. A city within a city, with its own schools, mosque, shops, markets, cottage industries…

The palace itself is lovely: a series of large, airy pavilions surrounded by graceful foliage, the whole aspect being one of openness and informality. Of course, the pavilions themselves are elaborately (and actually quite unaesthetically) carved, but they have little of the formal grandeur of palace architecture, generally. Even the royal collection of objects is modest—apart from the absolutely superb batiks, which are enough to make a visit to the palace well worth your while.

There was a dance performance of some kind going on in the first pavilion, but we gave it a miss. Have never been one for Javanese or Balinese dancing—really, it's much too slow and stylised for me.

From the palace we rode, on our *becak*, through the really pretty streets in the palace compound. Low-rise, single-storey dwellings with tiled roofs, greenery spilling over all around, hibiscus and frangipani and canna and orchids in such abundance, filling the air with fragrance and delighting the senses. Not a trace of glass and concrete anywhere. What a difference this makes to a cityscape, and how accustomed we have grown to its dominating presence everywhere else in the world. I daresay Jakarta is like Kuala Lumpur and Manila and Bangkok and Penang and Mumbai, and so on, but Yogya is definitely different. Its scale is human and much more likeable.

What struck us again and again is the absence of any overt poverty in both Yogya and Bali. No beggars, no obsequious hustling, nothing shifty or shady about any of the tourism ancillaries that we encountered. It's obviously not a rich society—in Ubud we were amazed that a commercial laundry charged us the equivalent of USD 1.50 to wash and iron eight to ten garments. Clearly salaries are low, the money made from tourism doesn't really benefit the locals—like everywhere else in the world—so how do people sustain themselves? The same is true of the hundreds of kiosks everywhere, hawking the same tourist junk. How on earth could they possibly profit from their sales? Most people shrug them off, we seldom saw anyone actually buying something from their shops, so—it's a real mystery.

At our *becak* driver's suggestion we went to the Government Batik Arts Centre which has students of batik art demonstrate the art every weekend. The paintings were exquisite, and you realise just how crude and undeveloped our batik is in India. No comparison. We saw such fine examples of Javanese and Balinese, but especially Javanese, batik that we were filled with awe and admiration.

Pogey insisted on walking down Yogya's main street, amusingly named Marlioboro (after the Duke), and really, if Prawirotaman is Paharganj, then M'boro is Ajmal Khan Road. Definitely worth a miss. Nothing but cheap junk, acres of motorbikes and food stalls. Nope, not for me.

Back at the Ministry, we decided to check out the highly recommended Omar Duwur restaurant for dinner. It's certainly a very elegant and beautifully sited place, but the food wasn't up to expectations. Donny's repast was far, far superior. Goes to show, I suppose, that you can't always go by what the guidebook says. I must say, though, that the glazed banana dessert was lovely...

No sooner had I got ready in the morning than I sprained my back again—a chronic cross I have to bear. That tell-tale twinge could only be a muscle spasm. Shit. Just when we were about to begin the fun part of our holiday in Bali. What to do? Trust in Johnson's Capsicum Plaster, Volini, painkillers—and a fervent prayer! Bit of a bore though, if it meant not being able to walk around...

We arrived in Bali armed with our *Lonely Planet* and oodles of advice from Katia, our Paris friend who's a Bali junkie, about what to do, where to go, whom to meet! Tried telling her gently that this was supposed to be a holiday, that we didn't want to rush around seeing performances and temple ceremonies, but she handed us maps and performance schedules and flyers from massage and beauty parlours—and a list of her favourite cafés in Ubud! 'And you call Rana (Kunang's sister) as soon as you arrive. And Rio, too, he's a big photographer and his studio is on the same street as the suckling pig place…near the palace.'

Ubud is an hour's drive from Denpasar, and lives up to all the superlatives used to describe it. Everything, from the paddy-fields and lotus pools to the vegetation—frangipani and palm trees, orchids, heliconia that is 10 ft high, red, yellow, orange and white hibiscus and flower offerings everywhere—stuns the senses and fills you with delight. It's just so gorgeous. (The fruit, on the other hand, is surprisingly tasteless. You'd think the pineapple and papaya and watermelon would be sweet and flavourful, but no. Only the bananas are good.) It reminded me of the best of Coorg and Kerala, a heady combination of the two, but so developed for tourism as to seem a bit like Bellagio. After the initial impact, a bit unreal. But it's the only place in the world we've been to where the farming takes place at your doorstep—literally—and rice-fields creep right up to the sidewalk. Everywhere. There's no real distinction between 'town' and 'country', between inside and outside. It makes for a marvellous continuity and, I do believe, is one major reason for the great feeling of tranquility one experiences. You'll be sitting in a café, drinking your coffee in ultra trendy surroundings, but turn around and a farmer will be transplanting paddy less than fifty yards away. From our room in the hotel, we actually observed the paddy grow during the week we were there!

The hotel! Bungalows, really, in a most salubrious setting, with the largest, most comfortable room and bathroom I have ever been in. (Except, maybe, for the room in the Galle Face in Colombo.) A wide and deep veranda with a mini bar and a mini kitchen that opened onto the paddy-fields as far as the eye could see. You could walk straight from the room into the paddies. All around was the same abundant foliage as on the rest of the island. We couldn't have asked for anything more.

Ubud is a series of villages strung together, and Greenfields, our hotel, was in Pengosekan. Used to be quite poor originally but is near the centre of Ubud, so very prosperous. As is the whole of Bali. Tourism it appears, has been responsible for all the infrastructure on the island—roads, 24-hour electricity, telecommunications, but very little medical or educational improvement. So the maximum benefit of all this revenue expenditure goes to the tourism industry—and the tourists. Six million a year, we're told, compared to two or three million for the whole of India!

Like tourists everywhere, we stilled our conscience and settled in happily in our very congenial Bale (room) Bintang.

'We'll take it easy', said Pogey next morning, in deference to my back. 'Just walk around a bit, see the main street, that's all.' That walk ultimately extended to five hours and almost 10 km as we wandered along Monkey

Forest Road, Ubud Raya, the Sultan's Palace, then down Hanoman Road and back to Pengosekan. Along the way stopping at boutiques and batik shops, gawking at shop windows, pausing for lunch at a restaurant where the view was wonderful and the food awful—and then entering the Sultan's Palace.

What an amazing environment! At times it was difficult to tell the pavilions from the foliage, so intertwined had they become. Like the palace in Yogya, this, too, was open to the elements, set amid trees and palms and flowering plants—and never mind that Rana Helmi, the next day, gasped in horror and said it was 'dreadful'! Kitschy and pretentious. Yes, if you saw only the hideous furniture and overwrought Garudas and frilly antimacassars on the sofas…But that was not all there was to it. The patina on the pavilions, the pools of water, the lotuses and frangipani all combined to lend it grace and unusual beauty. Agreed, without the extraordinary magic of the environment it would have made a very different impression. But then, it wouldn't have been in Bali, would it?

The really nice thing about Ubud is that homes and temples and shops and cafés are all part of each other. Many cafés have a temple right next to them—Rana Helmi has one in her compound—and each seems to be an extension of the other. Everywhere there are offerings on palm-leaf confections, they are made several times a day and can be seen on doorsteps, outside shops and hotels, everywhere. And one begins to think that Rio Helmi may be right: the Balinese are preoccupied with the ritual and ceremony of Hinduism, not its philosophical or intellectual content.

Wherever we went, people asked us whether we were Hindu. It was an important identification. Meant little to us, but established a kind of legitimacy to the enquirer. Dewa Made Santana, the owner of Greenfield Bungalows, couldn't hide his disappointment at our obvious lack of 'spirituality'—too 'modern' he thought, sadly—but it wasn't just Santana. Rana and Rio Helmi are practising Buddhists; Rio has even had a stupa constructed in his garden, so it must be that there's something in the air. Maybe Hindu Bali has to assert itself in predominantly Muslim Indonesia. Maybe it's still a very religious society. It's very likely that the 'modernity' we see is rather superficial…

Rio Helmi is a well-known photographer—listed among the world's hundred best, his sister Rana informed us—with a gallery on (as Katia said) the same street as the suckling pig food stall! He invited us to lunch and it was a most interesting experience. We arrived at his gallery and saw some of the photographs of Bali (and India, he comes here often) that have made him so famous. Very striking, in a Felix Roiter/Raghu Rai kind of way. (And, in fact, he told us that Raghu Rai was a good friend.) Sort of *National Geographic*-y.

Rio and Rana are Javanese, but have lived in Bali since the mid-1980s. Both are into Tibetan Buddhism, and Rio is a regular at Dharamsala. His house in Ubud is one of the most beautiful I have ever seen. He has two units: one three-bedroom one which he lives in, and another two-bedroom one which he lets out. Both are a composition of elegant pavilions (the traditional Balinese *bale*) set in a kind of L around lotus pools, a swimming pool (each!) and verdant greenery. Simply but very well-furnished, the whole exuding a serenity that is hard to describe. Rio has constructed a Buddhist stupa in one corner of his garden, and next to it is a Bodhi tree, grown from a sapling he brought from Sri Lanka—which, in turn, was from a tree that grew from the original Bodhi tree in Bodh Gaya. Whether it did or not, Rio's tree is a beautiful specimen.

Lunch was delicious. Vegetarian, lightly cooked brown rice, a very fresh salad with cottage cheese, and Balinese coffee. Oh, and an Indonesian cinnamon cigarette, courtesy Rana, who joined us later.

From their conversation we got a perspective on Bali that was both useful and informative. It's a remarkably homogenous society, and a remarkably religious one, too. Over the days that we encountered this in one way or another, we began to see the point of Rio's observation made earlier. It's all about ceremony and ritual observance and daily offerings, but perhaps that is what gives them a shared sense of values? We were struck by something Rana said: there's virtually no crime in Bali, and should anyone be caught stealing, they will almost certainly be done to death by the community. Bit extreme that, but you get the picture. There's no pick-pocketing, you're completely safe on the streets, and all doors are kept open. It's very possible that this is one reason why the Balinese have been able to resist the tourism assault of the last twenty-five years. It's also possible that television rather than tourism (as Dewa Made Santana believes) will be a more pernicious influence.

Rana herself is more than religious, hers being a religion of choice and conviction. Like Rio she is a serious Buddhist, and in fact, said that all she wished for was uninterrupted time devoted to its study. Survival needs, however, compel her to interrupt her study time with assignments that she does for money (mainly translations) and costume design on order. She showed us photographs of some exquisite jackets she has made with fabric specifically created or printed for the job. Some wonderful batik made by an American expatriate, banana-leaf fabric in muted gold… lovely stuff.

It was when she began speaking about communicating with the dead, and the common belief among the Balinese that the dead return in another body to their original families, that we began to feel a bit uneasy. Reluctantly, because it was so peaceful sitting there and conversing, we said our goodbyes and left.

A curiously satisfying encounter in an unexpected way.

We spent the afternoon ambling on Ubud Raya, west of the palace, but these streets in Ubud offer more of the same: acres of awful tourist souvenirs, some gems of batik—fabric and art ('mostly new, yeah, mostly new,' said Santana) and scores of cafés. How they all survive is a mystery. In all the time that we were there, we never saw more than a couple of tables that were occupied—except on our last evening, when both Café des Artistes and Casa Luna were choc-a-bloc. Didn't get a chance to sample the fare at the former, but Casa Luna (owned by an Australian woman, who is also the organiser of the Ubud Writers' Festival) was frankly, bad. Pre-cooked frozen food, heated to lukewarm temperature and dished out. Like Murny's Warung, where we had eaten a couple of days earlier.

'You should see Gunung Kawi, if you can,' Rana had said, 'it's an archaeological site, and the journey to it is very interesting. Stop at Gunung Batur on the way if you like.'

Gunung Kawi is the site of an eleventh-century memorial consisting of ten massive sculptures set in hillside caves, north of Ubud, in the town of Tampa Siring. Cut into the sheer cliff-face they tower to a height of seven metres, and are believed to commemorate one member of Balinese royalty, each.

The memorial is set in the most extraordinary environment—a deep, deep valley, surrounded by terraced rice-fields, thick jungle and tropical vegetation. You descend to it by way of steep steps, till you finally reach the monument, past which rushes a fast-flowing stream. It's the environment more than the monument itself, which is arresting, really, because the shrines are fairly unremarkable. Some archaeological significance, though, which I suppose is justified.

A very welcome coffee at the Kafe Kawi, with a fantastic view of the surroundings, a fifteen-minute interlude, and we were on our way to the volcano of Gunung Batur and the lake named after it.

I've never seen a volcano from up close before, and the experience was truly exhilarating. Gunung Batur is in the central mountains of Bali, is still active, and in the past has had two major eruptions—in the 1920s, when the village of Batur was completely submerged, and again in the 1960s, with a milder eruption. We were actually in the crater itself, on its rim initially, and then at its very centre, with its cones disappearing and reappearing as the mist descended and lifted. The sides of the volcano were black with laval soil, all around us was strewn aeons of volcanic rock, and warnings that volcanic activity was possible at any time. It was a bit eerie, but actually, very exciting to be in the volcano's crater, and I would have loved to trek up to the big cone, if possible.

Since it wasn't possible, we contented ourselves with watching the beautiful Lake Batur curving around one side of the cone. It's a large lake, and reminded me of Wast Water in the Lake District. We ate lunch at a restaurant perched above the lake, so had a lovely unobstructed view of it, and of the village as it has now been relocated to the outer rim of the volcano. Pogey had a surprisingly excellent meal, the fish of the day from Lake Batur, excellently flavoured, and I had an absolutely forgettable plate of spring rolls. Just my luck—or bad choice. It clearly wasn't my day for fine dining because dinner that evening at Murni's Warung was equally disastrous. But we did buy a lovely batik sarong for Pogey from their shop, a Javanese *parongberong* that he had been eyeing—and we saw the most stunning gold mask in Murni's collection. A Javanese ritual mask (we think) of extraordinary beauty. Thank goodness looking is free, because it was really expensive.

As Ratna said when we were planning our trip, there's not much to see in Bali apart from temples and rice-fields!

And since we weren't really that interested in temples (much to everyone's disappointment) we decided to relax and enjoy our leisure in Ubud, happy that for once, we didn't feel obliged to see all the sights. In the many galleries on Ubud Raya and Monkey Forest Road we saw some wonderful objects, mostly ritual or religious, or then Buddhas and Buddhist vajras, bells, Buddha's hands and so on. In the end, on an impulse really, we bought a very fine pair of hands in bronze, from Thailand, they said, exquisitely wrought. Somehow, those hands were of such compassion and grace that it was immensely comforting just to look at them.

On a more or less similar impulse the next day, we bought a marvellous tao-tao from Sulawesi, the erstwhile Celebes. Tao-tao are ritual sculptures, part of ancestor worship among the Toraja of Sulawesi. This one came complete with a crown of such sophisticated aesthetics, it was astonishing. A perfect crescent in copper, curving into a lizard's head at the end and perched on the tao-tao's head like a halo. Well, we fell for it and bought it. To be able to gaze upon it in wonder and amazement. I remembered the exhibition from New Ireland, one of the South Sea Islands, that I had seen at Paris' new Musée de Quai Branly. I don't think I have ever seen anything like it before. Scores and scores of stunning masks, bird masks, animal masks, human faces, mythical creatures; totemic figures over ten feet high; boats with rowers that occupied a whole room—you have to marvel not only at the power of the imagination, but at the beliefs that drive it. Wouldn't it be wonderful to visit Sulawesi…

Santana dropped in at our *bale* just as we were settling down to enjoy a morning of reading and doing nothing. He's a funny fellow, really. An astute businessman, running a successful hotel, a painter by inclination and training, deeply religious, and full of practical wisdom, if one can use that word uncynically. Lives modestly in his village, travels only on his motorbike, seldom leaves the island, and plans to retire and renounce the worldly life by the time he's in his mid-fifties. We didn't know whether to take him seriously. Says the vibes in his hotel are so peaceful (which they are) and positive because he made sure he observed all the necessary requirements for constructing a place like this. Made the right offerings, makes sure his staff are happy (runs the place most efficiently with only eighteen people), and will not double his capacity, though he can.

So what's the average income in Bali for, say, a shopgirl or waitress? About Rp 1,500,000 or USD 165, he said. Same as in India, approximately, but here people may work at two or three jobs if they are self-employed or in the private sector. And there's no stigma attached to any kind of labour. (In fact 90 per cent of the population is Sudra, so there are none of the caste hierarchies of India on the island.) And because there's no separation between farm and non-farm, a man may, if he wants, drive a taxi in the morning, work in the rice-fields in the afternoon (or vice versa) and wait at a restaurant in the evening.

Santana also maintains that the gap between the very rich and the modest sections of society is not that great, or visible. Of course there are rich Balinese, but there's little ostentation, and lifestyles are generally simple. So what do the wealthy do with their money? 'Spend it on temples,' he laughed, 'on more elaborate offerings and ceremonies.'

So many islands still to see in this archipelago, Sumatra and Sulawesi, even other parts of Java…

As the touts and guides and *becak* drivers in Java said, maybe later.

Egypt: Revolution in an Ancient Land

November 2011

Tahrir. Now an iconic space, almost as hallowed as the Cairo Museum that is situated at one end of the square or, rather, circle. That first evening, on the way to Zamalek from the airport, we had to cross it, of course, but would have gone there anyway to see it for ourselves. Evening crowds, families, young men, lots of them, out at the day's end, older men sitting with their hookahs, playing dice, kibitzing. Women with children strolling, hawkers hawking, balloons dotting the sky. In one corner a largish knot of people are listening to an impromptu speech, but we can't make out what it's about, and Hamad, Ahdaf's driver, doesn't know either. Not a planned meeting, it seems, unlike the demonstration outside the Arab League offices where people are protesting against Bashar Assad.

Ahdaf divides her time between London and Cairo, writing her books, newspaper columns, and organising PalFest, the Palestine Literature Festival. She had booked us into the Horus hotel, also in Zamalek (where she lives)

The Temple at Karnak

and a favourite with writers and artists. This time, it was just Pogey and me in Egypt.

Zamalek, a little island of leafy green streets, fashionable shops, the posh oasis in a city of eighteen million. Omar or Robbie, Ahdaf's son, dismissively refers to its rich denizens as *fulouls*—the irrelevant ones. The counter-revolutionaries. Robbie, a filmmaker, was an active participant in the January 2011 revolutionary, youth-led protests in Tahrir, and now works in an alternative media collective that produces material to counter the misinformation put out by the state. And the military. Misinformation like the deliberate lies around the shooting of Copts in Maspero, in old Cairo, on 9 October. Unofficial video footage that Robbie and his friends managed to get hold of established that the military opened fire first on a peaceful demonstration, for which the protestors had permission, and not that they were attacked by an unarmed crowd. Deaths resulted. Anger is growing. The general impression is that the military is creating the circumstances which will allow them to claim a state of chaos and declare a postponement of the elections, due to begin on 28 November 2011.

No, things are far from positive in this Arab Autumn in Cairo as far as the political situation is concerned. The military appears to be in for a long haul, the US is far from unhappy with that, and there's no real organised political opposition, apart from the Muslim Brotherhood—but the Americans have said they can comprise no more than 30 per cent of an elected government.

So, is this the outcome of President Hosni Mubarak's

exit? Did the revolutionaries simply do the military's job for it: oust Mubarak so that they could step in without a coup? They were never too happy with Mubarak, anyway, especially after his attempts at sidelining the military in favour of the police, and replacing senior military officers as ministers with business cronies, thus doing them out of lucrative sinecures.

Some of this will be part of Ahdaf's personal/political memoir of the heady eighteen days in January–February 2011 that she was writing, called *Cairo: My City, Our Revolution*, due for publication on 19 January 2012, marking the first anniversary of the revolution. That morning, news of Colonel Gaddafi's assassination had simultaneously closed and opened a chapter in next-door Libya's eight-month long bloody revolution.

Ahdaf decided we needed to put all this political stuff out of our minds for the moment and spend our first evening in Cairo in the historic Islamic part of the city. Well, it took us a good long while to get there because we were stuck in the mother of all traffic jams, which continued for kilometres! We just crept along, inch by inch, as pedestrians hurried past, but for sheer liveliness of street life it was hard to beat. Pavement vendors, food and bric-a-brac, hardware, all manner of kitsch, like any market square in old cities, bustling with busy-ness. When we got to the old Islamic quarter eventually, it was positively quiet by comparison. Lovely old mosques and residences restored with sensitivity, wide streets, very clean—and, compared to Chandni Chowk, very orderly. The same streets, divided by wares—gold, silver, textiles, pottery, spices—but walking was a pleasure, not an obstacle race. And the jaalis on buildings, both wooden and stone, were simply beautiful.

Back into town for dinner, at a restaurant with character—Estoril, something of a hangout for academics, students, arty types, where we had a most satisfying meal of short eats and salads. But by this time, we were practically falling asleep on our feet as it was almost 3 a.m., Delhi time!

The next morning Hamad dropped us off at the Cairo Museum, where we spent the next few hours being gobsmacked by the most stupendous collection of art in the world. And not just the art, but the sophistication, skill and imagination of a civilisation that could produce such wonder 5,000 years ago. Monumental, colossal, minute, filigreed—in stone, clay, gold, wood, cloth, alabaster. Every material they could find, precious or semi-precious, they wrought with breathtaking confidence and brilliance. And then the hieroglyphics, the pictorial and the abstract in compositions that seem 'modern' in their arrangement and aesthetic. We moved from one magnificent example to another, from the resplendent glory of Tutankhamun to the mummies, bandaged and embalmed, their viscera in elaborate alabaster jars, representations of a worldview so complete and, yes, confident in itself that you can only marvel at it. It struck me then that, really, technological advance apart, have we really accomplished anything comparable? Who will wonder at us, thousands of years from now? And if this was our experience at the museum, how could we possibly anticipate Luxor?

Nothing could have been a greater contrast to the drama and scale of the exhibits at Cairo Museum than what we experienced later that afternoon in Coptic Cairo. Getting off the Metro at Mar Girgis we stepped into an environment of such calm and tranquility that it took us quite by surprise. Very few tourists—partly because of the shootings in Maspero earlier in the month, but also, I suspect, because not many tour operators bring their busloads to see the Coptic churches, the synagogues or the Coptic Museum.

This is the heart of Egypt's indigenous Christian community, and its largest minority. A small Nile-side settlement, said to date back to the sixth century BC, seems to have flourished here, and in the second century AD, the Romans built a fortress called Babylon in Egypt, which you see as soon as you step out of the Metro station. It's a handsome, very well-restored monument, as are the other ruins in the Coptic Compound. The locals think they are too self-consciously preserved, with an eye to 'beautification' for the benefit of tourists. Well, I can't argue with them on that, and if one doesn't care for all that spit-and-polish restoration one can always pop into the Church of St George or the Synagogue, which are sombre and beautiful and make no attempt to please—they are already gracious, serene, sacred. The evening azaan floated in the air as we entered the Church of St George, the beautiful recitation surrounding and flowing into the church on waves of pure and clear sound, flooding one's being with a profound sense of the sublime. The church itself is built on a promontory, and below it wind the alleys of the quarter, the sides of one such being lined with books on makeshift bookshelves. On Egypt, on art and architecture, in Arabic and English—and here, unexpectedly, Deniz Kandiyoti on gender, Ahdaf's novels, Denys Davies-Johnson's *Memories of Translation*, Naguib Mahfouz, of course, and several titles published by the American University in Cairo.

We wandered through the streets leisurely, stepping in and out of churches, restoration sites or just blind alleys, till we ended up at the Coptic Museum, which is beautifully installed and organised. Nevertheless, one is struck by how, several thousand years after the Pharaohs, modest and minor Christianity's artistic efforts were by comparison. Both imaginatively and aesthetically: after all, what was there up until the European Renaissance that could compare with what the Pharaohs, the Aztecs, the Incas, the Mayans, indeed, all the ancient civilisations, had to offer? So we admired the display and the intricate woodwork and painted and carved ceilings and delighted in the manuscripts, but really speaking, they were all dwarfed by Tutankhamun and Cheops and Amenhotep and Hatshepsut and…

In the evening we dined with Ahdaf who had invited her sister, Laila Soueif, a professor of mathematics at Cairo University; her aunt, Lulie, an oncologist in Alexandria; and her brother, Ala, an IT professional, and as they were all actively involved in the January revolution, naturally dinner table conversation was dominated by what was in store now, politically, with the elections around the corner.

Laila, a founder member of the Kefaya Movement, regaled us with stories of the ineptitude of the political parties scrambling to nominate candidates; wary of alliances with other parties but unable to make it on their own; united in wanting the military out but fumbling and floundering on strategy and direction. So much so, that none of the three presidential hopefuls, El Baradei included, wanted to run as part of a political group—they were standing as independent candidates. Even as we spoke and listened, Ahdaf's brother was presenting a restructuring plan for the bureaucracy to the Ministry of the Interior, in order to bring about the changes that the collapse of the Mubarak regime was supposed to accomplish. The mood that evening vacillated between pessimism and a kind of resigned compromise, which acknowledged the glaring shortcomings and reversals of the past two months, but believed in getting the political process going through the elections, however flawed. And in the meantime, expose, expose, expose the government through all the media means available to them.

It's such a complicated political context that it could either revert to business as usual or herald another round of resistance and protest—but this time with the anticipation of violence by the state.

It was strangely exhilarating, but also a little disquieting, this juxtaposition of an extraordinary ancient culture with an equally extraordinary contemporary political reality.

* * *

On our third day in Egypt, Ahdaf arrived at 10 a.m. and we set off for Giza and the pyramids. Five thousand years ago, Pharaonic Egypt spanned three centuries and thirty dynasties, divided into three kingdoms—old, middle and new. Ancient Memphis became the capital of a unified Upper and Lower Egypt at the point where the Nile Delta met the valley. The year was 3100 BC, and Memphis remained the capital till the seat of power shifted to Thebes (now Luxor) at the time of the New Kingdom. Pharaohs and pyramids go together but even so, the number of them scattered over Memphis is pretty staggering. Over a hundred, easily, with more being discovered every few years.

The great pyramid of Cheops at Giza is the largest in Egypt, 147 metres high, dated to around 2750 BC. It's true, no matter how much you think you can anticipate, the actual sight of the pyramids is pretty overwhelming. Their monumentality, of course, the massive stones that are piled up, one on top of the other, to enormous heights, the sheer geometry and engineering of these tombs is staggering. But it's the abstraction of the form, the perfection of the triangle, that impresses. The intersection of the finite and the infinite, the soaring of the soul into the cosmos, for if you extend the lines of the triangle upwards they will disappear into space. We've seen mausoleums and tombs of surpassing grandeur in many parts of the world, but I doubt that any of them is equal to the pyramids. (Unless it's the tombs in the Valley of the Kings…) Unlike on my earlier visit in 1997, this time I didn't climb (or rather crawl) up to the sarcophagus, but actually once you get up there it's a remarkably sombre space. Quite bare. What you realise though, is that you cannot even begin to imagine how they were built—and what's more, built to last. For several thousand years! The entire Nile Valley is dotted with these colossal tombs of which only a few now remain, but how amazing that they do.

We left this complex of three pyramids, gold stone against azure blue sky, and drove a short way further down to see the Sphinx, Cheops' half-lion, half-head-of-man (I mean king) statue, seated, with the pyramids as a backdrop. Considerably eroded now, the face is beautiful still, and the whole idea of combining the strength of the lion with the wisdom of man is pretty powerful.

Ahdaf's mother has a fruit garden a little beyond the pyramids in a village off the road to Mansouraiah; the term 'village' is a bit misleading as the entire road is urban, built up right till the turn-off to the villages, a cluster of modest dwellings, all pakka, some even two or three storeys high. Ahdaf's mother's house is situated in about two acres of garden, mostly date palm, lemon and mango trees, and a vine trellis over the courtyard. Palm trees in the courtyard, as well, their fronds a slatted umbrella filtering the sunlight. An air of cool quietude filled our beings as we sat in the courtyard eating fresh dates, succulent and honey-sweet. On the roof, the red and gold fruit was ripening or drying, and if you haven't tasted fresh dates you haven't really eaten dates.

From the garden we made our way further south to

Dahshour, the pyramid built by Cheops' father, said to be the first perfect pyramid in Egypt, thence to Ahdaf's friend, Sherif Borai's farm nearby. Dahshour is about 30 km south of Cairo, and it is only after you're well on your way there, more than halfway through the journey, in fact, that the urban sprawl gives way to the lush palm-studded greenery of the Nile Delta. The surprise is the desert, because sand and black soil are almost stuck to each other, so that within a kilometre inland of the green strip, there is nothing but sand as far as the eye can see.

We reached Dahshour just a little before it closed at 4 p.m., which was rather wonderful because we were the only ones there. Nothing but the three pyramids against sand and sky, in all their colossal glory, and us. It seems to me that this is the only way to see them, minus tourists sticking to them like barnacles and spoiling their perfection. Behind the perfect pyramid is the imperfect, bent one, abandoned before completion because the builder realised he had got the angle wrong—it rises in a curve, then rights itself sharply, acquiring something of a hump in the process. And a short distance away is a third, almost totally eroded pyramid, just a mound of mud-brick rubble now. Not all pyramids are timeless, I guess, and this one seemed to have succumbed to the stresses of life.

The light was slowly fading as we arrived at Sherif's farm, his little piece of heaven in the countryside, a refuge from 'the hell that Cairo has become'. Sherif is a one-man publisher, publishing books that he wants to, surviving on sales from just a couple of bookshops. Distribution is a 'disaster' in Egypt, he said (oh, familiar strains) and it's difficult for the books to get around, but he's obviously a man of some means or he couldn't have remained in business.

We sat in his garden, surrounded by date palms, frangipani and, yes, even a mango tree, where he served us a most excellent meal, cooked by himself. Zucchini, delicately flavoured and grilled, a delicious small chicken with tomatoes, potatoes and caramelised onion, baked rice, peas in tomatoes, and, of course, wonderful bread. The tomatoes were abundant this year, he said, and indeed they have been delicious wherever we've had them—bright red, juicy and rich. Oh, and the most delectable dessert of fresh dates baked with a little cream and liquor. Washed down with fresh pomegranate juice.

Darkness falls quite early these days, and as we talked, the birdsong ceased and the sky slowly filled with stars. The conversation turned—as it so often did when we were with Egyptians—to the elections and what they portend. Sherif is an idealist. He was at Tahrir every day during the January–February revolution, helped with money and other resources, and is passionate in his denunciation of the Supreme Council of Armed Forces (SCAF). It's a manipulative institution which will not relinquish power easily, he believes, will strong-arm the Muslim Brotherhood into a compromise alliance which will legitimise its authority and enable it to retain control of the country. The rest of the opposition, liberals, communists and others, he thinks are ineffective. Once installed, the government would be invulnerable because democratically elected, and the transformation that the revolution worked for, neutralised—or abandoned.

'So, what's your strategy,' asks Ahdaf, 'what should be the next step in the process?' 'More protests,' he says, 'continue the resistance and keep up the pressure till SCAF is dismantled and the army returned to the barracks.' There will be bloodshed this time, counters Ahdaf. Sherif agrees, but believes there will be blood on the streets anyway, should elections be held, but it will not be spilt in vain. His pessimism is shared by many, especially as alliances are being made and unmade every day. The Democratic Alliance for Egypt, which initially had more than thirty-four parties across the political spectrum and was the single largest bloc to contest the elections, had been reduced to ten—even the newly formed Islamist parties consisting mainly of the Salafists, had pulled out. Amir Hamzawi, professor of political science and a founder of the Freedom Egypt party maintains that one of the weaknesses of the Egyptian political elite is 'its inability to work collectively, manifested by the election and political alliances and struggle among parties over candidates' lists'. Unlike Tunisia, where power was transferred to a civilian authority, in Egypt authority passed to SCAF; moreover, many former members of the dissolved National Democratic Party are being fielded as candidates in the parliamentary elections, so that many seats might well be won by remnants of the Mubarak regime!

Meanwhile, the bureaucracy and governance are on

hold, the economy is sluggish, and tourism has been hit badly. And the one-word cause of it all is: Revolution.

* * *

Had a second taste of Cairo's notorious traffic snarls on our return from the Al Azhar Park and the Aga Khan Trust for Culture's (AKTC) restoration/rehabilitation work in the adjoining community of Darb-al-Ahmar. The Aga Khan has a special relationship with Egypt, his grandfather having fallen in love with Aswan when he visited it, and decided to be buried there when he died.

Al Azhar was a city garbage dump, all 30 km of it. Why not regenerate it? asked His Highness. But how? What about all the garbage? Well, where there's a will there's a way, as they say, and the Aga Khan's wish can become many people's command. So with the co-operation of the municipal corporation the garbage was shifted to a landfill site, three reservoirs were built and an extensive garden planted as a green lung for the city. It is an exemplary 'gift', as Sherif put it, a place of beauty and repose for the local inhabitants, as well as for a city with very few green spaces. The Park Director gave us a tour of the garden, remarkably mature for being only six years young, a superb lunch at their hilltop restaurant, and then took us to see the extensive restoration work that the AKTC has done, and is doing, in Darb-al-Ahmar. Mamluk and Ottoman, mosques and mausoleums, a secular building here and there, meticulously and beautifully restored in the manner of all AKTC projects. There's clearly an AKTC manual that all their offices are required to conform to, for we've seen the same results in Damascus, Aleppo, Delhi and, now, Cairo. It's certainly impressive, but the question of re-use recurs. You can't 'secularise' mosques and mausoleums, so what do you do once they're restored? Mosques can, of course, be opened for worship again but, as we were informed, there are thousands in the neighbourhood (including one used by a small Indian community of immigrants) so one more isn't an urgent necessity. Then, too, local residents aren't always amenable to being relocated while dwellings are being restored, and sometimes simply refuse to budge. Still, the AKTC has managed to upgrade several residences and, more importantly, has laid a sewage system and encouraged local crafts—metalwork and carpentry; there were lots of karkhanas buzzing (literally) with activity.

At dinner that evening, Ahdaf had invited her brother and sister-in-law, Sohair, as well as the writer, Radwa Ashour, and her son, Tamim Barghouti, a poet, and a few people from the British Council. The restaurant was the Charmerie in Zamalek, a lively Egyptian eatery with excellent food and atmosphere, even if a bit noisy! It was lovely to meet Radwa and Tamim, whom we had met in Washington earlier that year, again, and we drank to Radwa's latest award—the Nord Sud Foundation in Pescara had recognised her latest novel on the Palestine *naqba*, the only one of her novels to be published in Italian.

Tamim (who cannot vote in the forthcoming elections because he has not yet got Egyptian citizenship, his father being Palestinian) is back in Cairo, having resigned his teaching job at George Washington University. Like many other young Egyptians, he's immersed in the anti-military-SCAF resistance, his long poem on Tahrir has been recited and broadcast repeatedly on television so that he's a minor celebrity, not only as a resistance poet but as a rising star of classical Arabic poetry. This evening, though, it was his analysis of the equation between the Muslim Brotherhood and the military that was most incisive. Within the Brotherhood there is rebellion in the ranks, with younger members resenting the authoritarianism of the elders and their stranglehold on the organisation. (In Tunisia, apparently, the opposite prevails, with older members of the Ennahda party much more progressive than their younger conservative colleagues.) Desperate to keep the unity, the leadership will agree to any compromise with the majority party in the elections—as low as 20 per cent of the seats, according to Tamim—so that they retain their control over their flock.

In another conversation around the table, the discussion centred on the People's TV channel that media activists, intellectuals and the revolutionary youth planned to set up as an alternative news and information medium. To be publicly subscribed by the sale of shares ranging from €10 to a maximum of €30 per share. Whether and when they will get permission to do so is a moot question as all media, print and broadcast, are state-owned.

* * *

We left in the morning for Luxor, an hour's flight from Cairo. Luxor, seat of the Pharaohs of the New Kingdom (second century BC), of the grandeur of Thebes and the splendour of Karnak, the Valley of the Kings, the Temple of Hatshepsut, of Amon and Akhenaten and Amenhotep, all the Ramseses—and Tutankhamun. They stand on either bank of the Nile, with the Luxor Temple and Karnak on the East Bank and the others on the West. Thebes, or Upper Egypt (because the area is on the upper reaches of the Nile) is where the Pharaohs reached the height of their wealth and power. The rich Nile Valley soil, a consequence of annual flooding, afforded abundant agriculture, and the expansionist campaigns of Ramses II took him as far afield as Syria and Palestine. Vast empires require a vast bureaucracy, and the Pharaohs were served by an army of scribes and priests as well as labourers, potters, metalworkers, builders, artists, jewellers, weavers, butchers, fishermen, carpenters…all of whom, or at any rate many thousands of whom, were employed by the temples. As in India, the temples formed the heart of every settlement and were a place of worship, granary, town hall, college, library and medical centre. Granite was obtained from Aswan, sandstone from Gebel Silsila, alabaster from near Amarna, limestone from near Cairo. Gold came from mines in Nubia and the Eastern Desert, and copper and turquoise from Sinai.

We went straight to Karnak from the airport. The sun was high in the sky, the air was warm and quite still, the glare sharp—but, as a result, there were very few tourists. Hats planted firmly on our heads and eyes lowered to keep from squinting, we walked the few metres of open, unbuilt space towards the temple. When we raised our eyes, it was to take in the unforgettable, unimaginable sight of the massive pylons, soaring god knows how many metres high, and approached through an avenue of ram-headed sphinxes. You have to stop dead in your tracks because you cannot really take it in, can hardly believe the structure is still standing, its impact is so overpowering. First of all, the walls aren't straight, but at an incline of around 43 degrees, the same as the pyramid walls, which is supposed to give them stability. Then, you enter through a relatively narrow, but very high, space into a massive courtyard and are at once in the presence of giants. Huge statues of Amun, then the temples of Seti II, and that of Ramses III. You walk around slowly, eyes swivelling left and right, hardly able to move. Those statues have no equal—the scale, the solidity, the sublimity of expression, the sheer majesty—but as you proceed through the temple, you realise the whole complex is unequalled. Everything is gigantic. The site covers two kilometres, is made up of sanctuaries, kiosks, pylons, obelisks and huge pillars—the hypostyles—dedicated to the Theban gods and the greater glory of the Pharaohs. The guidebook says the Temple of Amun is the largest structure ever built (five centuries ago) and this is where the gods lived while on earth. Karnak was built, added to, dismantled, restored, enlarged and decorated over nearly 1500 years, and was the most important place of worship in Egypt during the New Kingdom. The priests of the Temple of Amun employed 81,000 people, owned 421,000 heads of cattle, sixty-five cities, eighty-three ships and 276,400 hectares of agricultural land. You can believe it.

When you enter the Great Hypostyle Hall, a forest of 134 towering papyrus-shaped stone pillars, your senses simply reel—disbelief is paramount. How on earth could they have first conceptualised, and then erected this monumental grouping, symbolising a papyrus swamp? Then, having built it, how on earth had they carved every square inch of its intricate detail, perfectly proportioned, not a line out of place, not a single wrong move? All kinds of scenes and vignettes, like Hindu temples, actually—everyday life, royalty, festivals, sacrifices, flora and fauna. History and geography, art and architecture, in divine and sublime harmony. You keep looking up and up, those flowering papyruses climb higher and higher, and your neck remains craned for almost the entire time you spend at Karnak. You turn a corner and run into Hatshepsut's Obelisk, thirty metres high (can't look down), its tip originally covered in electron, an alloy of gold and silver also used on the pyramids. You turn another corner and collide with a few huge fallen statues, move on and come up smack against an amazing frieze, which thankfully, is mostly at eye level. It takes a while to walk along it because it's almost as long as it's high.

One thing struck me about all the carving: it's exceptionally detailed yet remarkably spare in execution. Minimal, you could say. Nothing florid or fussy about it, clean lines, very little embellishment. And from what an untrained eye can tell, it continued like this through the centuries and dynasties. Not much evolution of style, just minor variations, it remained much the same for over three millennia. The explanation, it turns out, is simple: Egyptian art was functional, the majority of objects and artefacts, especially those produced for religious or funerary purposes, might never see the light of day. One feature is particularly charming—the nose and mouth needed to be shown in profile so that the figures could breathe, the eyes shown whole, to allow them to see. Eyes were also often painted on the sides of coffins to enable the dead to look out. Well, this not-for-display may be part of the reason for the Pharaonic style but it couldn't be the only one, because even its very public statues of gods and kings have the same spare, unembellished but powerful aesthetic, too sophisticated to be merely functional.

But why this preoccupation with papyrus? It's on every temple frieze, in every building, in full flower or bud (in which form it's clearly phallic) but it's only a plant, after all. Tamim, when I asked him later, had this to say: papyrus was the medium through which everything of importance was communicated, and on which all inscriptions, wars, victories and the glories of the Pharaohs were recorded. Next to the Pharaohs in the power hierarchy were priests and scribes, both of whom wrote these histories. The papyrus symbolised power and knowledge, combining in the figures of the god-kings.

The Old Kingdom Pharaohs were buried in tombs made to look like mountains, the pyramids, but by the time the New Kingdom moved south to Thebes, they were tunnelling into mountains already there, burrowing hundreds of metres deep into the earth to make a final resting place for the body. The Valley of Kings on the West Bank of the Nile at Luxor has sixty-three magnificent royal tombs from the New Kingdom (1550–1069 BC). Why the West Bank? Because the sun sets on the west and the setting sun was associated with the afterlife. (Indeed, Nut, the star-spangled goddess of the sky, swallows the sun every evening and gives birth to it the next morning.) Some tombs have been known since Greek and Roman times but the last one to be discovered, No. 63, was excavated as recently as 2006—and excavations for others are continuing.

You realise just how close you are to the desert in the Valley of the Kings—an endless vista of sand, broken only by sand-coloured low mountains, not a tree or green thing in sight, the sun beating down, the only shade being under your hat or umbrella. It's a relief to enter the tombs which are opened by rotation, to prevent damage due to over-exposure. The tomb of Ramses III, the last of the warrior kings of Egypt (1184–1153 BC) is one of the longest in the valley, and much of it is still beautifully decorated. It was the first one we entered, and as soon as you walk in, you know that you are in the presence of something awesome. The tomb enfolds you, encompasses and surrounds you, but far from being claustrophobic it is an astonishing and uplifting experience, because all around and above you is LIFE. Everything a soul might need in its passage to the afterlife, every instruction, every companion, every artefact, accompanying him as he makes his way through the stages of dying into life. Every inch of wall and ceiling is covered with the superb graphics of the *Book of the Dead*, the colours as fresh as if they were painted last week. Lustrous yellows and deep reds, skies so blue you could drown in them, greens from emerald to leaf…Black (the colour of the fertile black Nile soil) was the colour of life. This was complemented by the colours of stone chosen—white alabaster, golden sandstone, green slate, brown quartzite, black and red granite. Objects could be made of red or yellow jasper, blue lapis lazuli, orange carnelian. Copper, gold, silver. Wood and blue ceramic. Even as the colours dazzle and sparkle, the imagination runs wild visualising the rich treasures that lay in the tombs and were such a temptation to thieves and vandals. Another reason to delve deeper and deeper into the mountains and elude marauders.

The *Book of the Dead* gives way to funerary scenes, scenes of the Pharaohs in the company of gods, banquet scenes, each figure thought capable of containing the spirit of the person it represented. And more, and more…

Tomb after tomb after tomb, till you can't take any more. You *can* actually have too much of a good thing. After the Valley of the Kings, you need to go away somewhere quiet where you can try and absorb everything you've seen, slowly. Recall that last impression of the gigantic statue of Ramses II at Karnak in the dying light of day. Imagine how Howard Carter must have felt when he opened Tutankhamun's tomb and was dazzled by all that gold, the astounding treasure, chambers full of it.

Remember, too, that these were the riches in the tomb of an eighteen-year-old—what might they have found if he had died much later?

But we didn't go somewhere quiet, we made our way to the Temple of Hatshepsut (1400s BC), the only female Pharaoh, in Deir al Bahri, also on the West Bank. The temple rises sheer up into the mountain, is carved into it in three stages, so you walk up ramps onto the first courtyard and so on up to the third, and it has the same massive columns and vast spaces as the other temples. But—and this you really have to imagine because they aren't all there—the last terrace had twenty-four enormous statues of Osiris, god of the underworld, all in a row. You can just visualise them against the backdrop of mountain and sky, what an awesome sight they must have been, but there are only three or four left standing now.

Quite overwhelmed by the utter (and literal) enormity of what we were seeing, I was trying hard to telescope back so many thousand years, picture the temple as it had been then with nothing around it for miles. Just the 300-metre-high limestone mountains, the endless desert, the sacred rituals and observances it would have held, the flares of torches as they lit up the avenue of sphinxes that led to the temple. Processions of people, the sound of drums and cymbals, incense burning, the soaring chants of a thousand voices resounding in the night, then dispersing…

It was at the Luxor Temple that night that we experienced the consummate theatricality of the Theban temple, in all its drama and majesty. You're not really prepared for it because the temple is smack in the middle of town with everything swirling around it, noisily, ceaselessly. Not like the Valley of the Kings or even Karnak. There's an avenue of sphinxes all right, but you approach it from the temple, rather than advancing towards the temple from the avenue. So you wander in sort of casually and then, my God, your breath is sucked right out of you. You've passed through the enormous pylons and entered the first court and all around you, surrounding you, lit from below, highlighted but also in shadow, are the colossal standing and seated figures of Ramses II, surrounded by a double row of columns with lotus bud (not papyrus!) capitals. All decorated, with scenes of the Pharaohs making offerings to the gods, for this was the temple where the statues of the Theban triad, Amun, Mut and Khonsu were reunited with Amun of Opet. Luxor was where the sacred barque festival of Opet took place over four to six weeks every summer, when the statues were carried in procession in barques from Karnak to Luxor.

Walking slowly from the great court of Ramses II through the magnificent older Amenhotep Colonnade, we came at last upon the quiet space that we had been looking for all day. The Sun Court of Amenhotep is vast, it's surrounded on three sides by towering papyrus-bundle columns—and it's empty. You can sit in one corner, hidden by shadows, the night sky above you, the light from the lamp throwing the columns into sharp relief. Here, with the city teeming and pulsating outside its walls, was a place of such repose that we felt becalmed, enfolded by the temple. As if we were the only people in it. With Ramses, of course...

Back in Cairo the next evening, we were pulled up sharp by the news that Ahdaf's nephew, Alaa, Laila's son, had been summoned to the military court to be interrogated for some offence he was supposed to have committed at a demonstration the previous week, against the military firing and killing of twenty-eight Coptic Christians in Maspero. Alaa was accused of 'inciting violence' through his blogs and 'damaging military property'. Of course, he was also part of the campaign, 'No to Military Trials' spearheaded by his sister, Mona, which resisted the interrogation and trial of civilians by a military court. He was to be prosecuted on 30 October, a Sunday, but that Friday, the 28th, there would be a rally in his support at Tahrir, to coincide with a planned protest against the torture and death in custody of a poor labourer picked up on a drug-related charge. Increasingly, it seemed to be SCAF that was guilty of criminal action against ordinary citizens, but who would try them?

We couldn't participate in that demonstration because we were in Alexandria—but, there, too, people were out on the streets, and at the prestigious Bibliotheca Alexandrina the entire staff was on strike, demanding the resignation of the Director, Suzanne Mubarak's 'puppet'. They had managed to shut down the library, but showed up every day and sloganeered and declaimed on the premises, accompanied by revolutionary songs composed during the eighteen days between 25 January–11 February 2011. We were quite shocked by the huge disparity in salaries that the strikers were protesting: €66,000 (or USD 11,000) per month to the Director, but only €1500 (or USD 200) to the Librarian, and as little as €300 to the security staff. And at Cairo University, Radwa told me, a full professor's salary is €6000 (or USD 1000) per month, but the Vice Chancellor earns close to a million. 'Institutionalised robbery,' she said, because a new ruling apportioned a small percentage of the fee charged by every faculty in the university to each student—upwards of 300,000—as the VC's share! Mubarak's scheme for buying loyalty.

We looked in vain for Lawrence Durrell's and Constantine Cavafy's Alexandria (though we stayed at the Cecil, war-time base for Churchill and the British Secret Service, as well as the favourite haunt of Somerset Maugham and E.M. Forster and Noel Coward), but realised that theirs had been a largely Orientalist fantasy superimposed on a colonial European project. Egyptian Alexandria has little to do with the effete Europeans of the Alexandria Quartet, or its imagined 'natives'—although I suppose Cavafy's romance with the city was real enough for him. Even the city's few Graeco-Roman ruins are slender pickings. We were disappointed, except for the sweep of the Corniche and the splendid vista it afforded of the Eastern Mediterranean. That was wonderful.

On 30 October, Alaa was remanded to military custody, handcuffed and led into prison. He had refused to answer the prosecutor's charges, saying that SCAF, as an accused itself for the killing of innocent civilians, could not turn interrogator. It had no locus standi. Fifteen days of detention were followed by another fifteen, up to a maximum of forty-five days before his trial could commence. He was in his late twenties, expecting his first child that November. His father is one of the most highly regarded human rights lawyers in Cairo, but Alaa's decision to challenge the legitimacy of the charges against him had been a family consensus. The issue was larger than Alaa, they said, it was against military courts and they would mobilise against it with greater fervour. On Monday, 31 October, a rally of more than 3,000 people gathered at Tahrir, and twenty-two lawyers pledged support to Alaa, said they would appear on his behalf and ask for bail when his appeal was heard on 3 November. The court of the military prosecutor rejected his appeal and Alaa was handcuffed and imprisoned again.

Less than one week later, the interim government appointed by SCAF said it would impose a 22-article charter of 'principles' that would be binding on the committee appointed to draft a new constitution. It would prohibit parliament from supervising the military budget, and would also declare it the 'protector of constitutional legitimacy'. Moreover, under the new plan, the military would nominate eighty of the 100 members of the proposed constituent assembly—only twenty would be from among elected parliamentarians. Other provisions gave the army the right to reject any constitutional article it disapproved of, and to dissolve the constituent assembly if it did not produce a document that the army approved of within six months. On 18 November, the Muslim Brotherhood came out in strength in Tahrir, ostensibly to pressurise the military into diluting the provisions of this charter, especially with regard to protecting constitutional legitimacy. They saw this as the spectre of secularism disguised as a safeguard. Liberals and revolutionaries kept away and the demonstration was largely peaceful. But the very next day, Saturday, 19 November, activists and others in the tens of thousands thronged the square to protest SCAF's intentions and demand its immediate withdrawal from the government. The full force of the police rained bullets and batons on them; to the more than 1,000 dead in the January–February struggle were added another thirty-five, with several hundred injured. And Alaa was still in jail.

Watching from the sidelines, one couldn't help thinking that the eighteen-day Egyptian Spring had morphed into what could be a very long winter of discontent.

Turkey: Loitering with Intent

June 2015

You could, up until fifty years ago, carve out a cave dwelling for yourself in Cappadocia if you so wished. It could be a three or six or even nine million-year-old 'house', depending on which era of rock you chose—that's when the massive rock formations were thrown up across the region, when the three volcanoes that ring the valley, erupted 700 times.

The eruptions, about thirty million years ago of Erciyes and Hasan Melendiz Daglari, are responsible for the dramatic landscape of Cappadocia; they produced the region's raw material, tuff (porous rock formed by the consolidation of volcanic ash), covering the plateau of Urgüp with ash and mud. Centuries of erosion and settlement resulted in the formation of its towering rock chimneys, scattered over the countryside and creating a surreal and fantastical landscape. This is the landscape that stuns you when you see it, a work in progress for millennia, a continuous process of erosion, settlement, collapse, a succession of valleys marked by huge rock chimneys, mushroom-capped, and by cave dwellings, everywhere you look.

The Ortahisar Castle in Ürgüp

It's hard to imagine that this plateau was once a huge lake. When the volcanoes first erupted under the lakes (in the upper Miocene epoch) they poured tonnes and tonnes of lava that formed the first layer of the plateau. Subsequent eruptions, the last about three million years ago, layered the mud, ash, lava and other materials to give the rocks that resulted their characteristic colouring—rose (red laterite), grey (iron), white (sulphur). On a clear day, and from a vantage point, you can see the Rose Valley rocks with their striations as clearly as if they had been painted on.

It is simply not possible to describe the Cappadocia landscape, it has to be seen to be believed. And even if you see it in photographs or documentary films, there is no way you can experience it without being there. There are rocks and there are rocks. And then there are the Cappa rocks. You take a walk down any road, into a valley, and it's a surround sound of rocks. Miles of them, just there, on your right or your left or ahead, soaring up, yet up close. You can reach out and touch them or climb them or enter any one of the thousands of cave dwellings that dot the entire region, or you can stumble onto an ancient church, early Christian—or a Hittite home, prehistoric. A French priest similarly stumbled onto the rock-cut churches in 1907 and ever since then, more and more churches, monasteries and homes are being discovered. At last count, there were 20,000 cave dwellings in Cappadocia and more are being found every year. They have been lived in for over 4,000 years by the Hittites, the early and later Christians, and by the Turks, till the government of Turkey took them over in the 1970s.

We had a little taste of (twenty-first-century) cave-living ourselves at the Hezen Cave Hotel in Urgüp.

There were six of us there. Ayesha Kagal and her nephew, Vivan; Bunny and Jon Page from London, and Pogey and me. Urgüp is in the heart of Cappadocia and the hotel is a renovated cave dwelling, like hundreds of others in the region. No one owns the hotels—they are leased by the government to individuals or groups in order to encourage tourism, which is now the mainstay of the region. Cappadocia's population is 300,000, of whom 50,000 are employed by the tourism industry. By extension, 150,000 people depend on it for their household income. A region that had been more or less isolated for thousands of years, is now humming with tourists, wi-fi, the Internet, minivans, SUVs, cafés and restaurants.

The rocks remain unmoved.

Right outside and across the way from our hotel is the imposing Ortahisar Castle rock, rearing up from the flatland around, and when we first set eyes on it the evening we arrived, its crown was tipped with the gold of the setting sun. We remained glued to the sight for a good long while, because you had to take it in. The jagged rock, uneven and rough, pitted with what looked like large holes, oddly window-like in appearance, and some quite large 'doorways'. How on earth could this be called a castle? But 'castle' in Cappa, we learnt later, is the term for a civic centre, or the centre of authority—originally, fortresses like Ortahisar were used thus in Byzantine times.

Later that evening we wandered down to the only café

close by, the Tandir Café, which afforded us a spectacular view of Ortahisar from its balcony. As the sky darkened one side of the castle was suddenly ablaze, as if lit by incandescence, and then as suddenly, was engulfed in shadow. As night fell, it was as if the rock receded into the past, restored to its primitive essence.

Tandir is the same as tandoor, with meats and breads baked in it in the same way that we do. We had a delicious dinner of Cappadocian fare—bôrek, a flaky pastry filled with a delicate cheese, a carrot and yogurt dip, succulent lamb shank, a very unusual stew, and the usual salads and rice.

Not all the rocks in Cappadocia are mighty and monumental, and as we walked around the next day we saw long stretches of what looked like rock dunes—soft, undulating waves, pale pink, not yet aged into rock hardness. They have, after all, been evolving for 60,000,000 years. But how did some of them acquire that distinctive mushroom-like shape, poetically called fairy chimneys? (In reality, rather phallic, actually.)

Vast plateaus of the region were covered with volcanic ash, and the accumulated ash eventually formed a soft layer of tuff. Over thousands of years, rainwater began to erode the softer layers but the harder basalt remained unaffected. Cones embedded in mushroom-like shapes formed on the tops of hills, and became the fairy chimneys that dot the countryside. Where such erosion didn't take place, vast valleys of rock gradually formed into canyons that extend for miles, one following from the other. They are an awesome sight, and it's no wonder that Cappadocia has been declared a World Heritage Site.

Well, that's all very well, but it boggles the mind to think that the rock caves were lived in till the 1970s. Not just lived in, but prayed in, painted in, apprenticed for the church in, hid in, and protected by. The soft stone made carving out spaces possible, and because the tuff does not absorb paint, the frescoes adorning the rock churches can still be seen.

The first humans in Cappadocia can be traced back to 500,000 years ago. The Hittites inhabited the region till the 1200s BC, followed by the Persians in the sixth century BC, who brought large parts of Anatolia under their control. Cappa became one of their thirteen provinces or satraps, and paid as taxes, 1,500 horses (the famous horses of Cappadocia), 2,000 cattle and 20,000 sheep, every year. Macedonians under Alexander replaced the Persians, then Julius Caesar, and after the Romans came the early Christians, fleeing the Roman armies. The caves of Cappadocia became their refuge, and Cappa itself offered a safe haven for the propagation of Christianity. (Some people maintain that the spread of Christianity can be traced to 330 AD, in Cappa.) Finally, the Turks from Central Asia conquered the area and brought in Islam.

In Göreme's Open Air Museum—a cluster of seventeen impressive rock churches and monasteries near Urgüp—you can see evidence of this growth through the first to the seventh century, when the Iconoclastic period saw the large-scale destruction and defacement of all images. What remains of the frescoes—which tell the story of Jesus, of course, but also of local saints—display a delicate palette of yellow, ochre and brown, those being the only colours that could be derived from the region's vegetation. The art is naïve but charming, and the subjects the usual ones found in churches across the world: the birth of Christ, the Three Wise Men, Christ's miracles, including the raising of Lazarus, the Stations of the Cross and the Crucifixion. Yet, if you think that the Ajanta cave paintings belong to the same period, and that just some hundreds of miles to the west of Cappa, the Romans and Greeks had built sophisticated temples and terrace houses and theatres at the same time, if not earlier, you realise just how isolated and primitive this region must have been. And, even in the most elaborate of the rock churches, the twelfth-century Tokali Church in Göreme with its detailed frescoes and rich colours, you cannot forget that you are in a cave.

There are over 700 rock churches in all of Cappadocia, some just modest family shrines. Around 330 AD the ruling king, in order to encourage the spread of Christianity, told the people that if they built such shrines they would be exempt from paying tax. This period coincided with the persecution of Christians in the Roman Empire, and many of them fled east to Anatolia and the cave shelters of Cappa. It was in these shelters that the early monasteries were founded.

But it's not only monks and priests and farmers and their families who lived in the caves, the pigeons of Cappadocia also had their own houses—and still do.

Pigeon Valley is studded with, literally, pigeon-holes in the rocks, where thousands of birds live. Every family in the valley has a pigeon-house, and pigeon eggs are collected twice a year to sell. In earlier times, the eggs were collected to be used as egg tempera for the frescoes; now pigeons are kept primarily because pigeon-droppings are used as manure for the fields. Up until the 1960s anyone could build a pigeon-house any time; in the 1970s and 1980s the government began an aggressive potato farming programme, which soon succumbed to extensive damage by potato pests. Pesticides killed the insects all right, but they also killed the pigeons that ate the insects. Pigeon deaths deprived the fields of manure, and farmers of one source of income.

For me, though, all this was quaintly interesting enough, but the real marvel was the landscape and the rocks. Every valley opened up a new vista, yet another wondrous formation, and even though Jon jadedly said, 'Rocks are rocks,' he was forced to admit in the end that, 'these rocks rock.'

We left the Open Air Museum of Göreme and made our way to Aranos, a village renowned for its pottery. Aranos' clay is special, and we were told that every man in the village had to be a potter or he wouldn't find a bride! In winter, when there was no farming to be done, the men potted and the women wove carpets. Ghalip of Chez Ghalip, is a master potter, and his family have been potters for 400 years. In his workshop, large cavernous rooms, we saw magnificent pieces made by his potters, some fired at 1000 degrees Centigrade for ten hours, hand-painted and glazed as they have been for hundreds of years, using the red clay from the bed of the Kizilirmak river, as their predecessors did in Hittite times.

When the Ottomans overran central Turkey and moved further west, up to the Aegean coast, they began a strategy of transferring Turks to their captured territory in Greece, and Greeks to Turkey, in an attempt to consolidate the Empire. There's nothing new about transferring populations, we realised, if you want a demographic dividend. The Greek village of Çavuşin, now abandoned, lies five kilometres from Göreme, and here the aspect is of dozens of connected cave houses across whole hillsides. The image is startling, and in the evening light, consists of a series of voids and mass, as openings in the hillside disappear into dark spaces which are the dwellings. Wandering in this uninhabited village is an oddly satisfying experience. Without the noise and bustle of tourist traffic one is free to imagine a way of life, however idiosyncratic that might have been, as recently as in the 1960s.

You can go for long pleasurable two-hour walks (we didn't) or look at some of Çavuşin's churches (we did). The cognoscenti will no doubt be able to discern subtle distinctions between early, middle and later cave churches, but to my inexpert eye they seemed more or less the same. No less interesting for that, though.

That quiet Çavuşin interlude ended with a wonderful fish lunch, at which Ayesha discovered the delights of Efes beer, the dark one. Sadly, not commonly available, as she found later.

In the afternoon we went to Kayamakli, one of thirty-six currently known underground cities in Cappadocia (there are said to be almost a hundred more!), and one of the largest in the region. As happened often, it started pouring just as we reached Kayamakli so it was a good thing we were under, rather than above, ground. Very far underground, as it turned out, 20 metres deep!

Kayamakli, located 20 km from Nevşehir, was discovered in 1964 and is dated to the early Byzantine era. Underground cities were of enormous value in the early Christian era, as they provided shelter for extended periods, to Christians who were being persecuted by the Romans. We were told that you could live in them for over two months at a time, with adequate provision of the four essentials: light, air, food and water. Later, we were able to see for ourselves how this was possible.

Underground cities were lived in from the earliest times—by the Hittites, who descended into them during the bitterly cold winter (the temperature in these cities remains an unvarying 11–17 degrees Centigrade, year round); by first-century Christians who hid from the Romans; and by eighth-century Christians who hid from the Arabs. Legend has it that when Persian and Arab armies set out to vanquish the Christians, beacons were lit and this advance warning could travel from Jerusalem to Constantinople in hours. When the message reached Cappadocia, the Byzantine Christians escaped via secret tunnels into the underground cities.

The softest points in the volcanic tuff were identified

in order to begin excavating the cities. As ventilation was crucial, the first things to be dug were ventilation shafts, some 70–80 metres deep. At the base of the shafts were wells for water, which would be transported up to the upper levels. We saw these incredible air shafts that were the oxygen cylinders for these vast cities, capable of holding 4,000 people at any one time. Smaller cities might accommodate only 150 families, but Kayamakli and Derinkuyu, the two largest, held many more.

Imagine, if you will, these extraordinary cities. You enter ordinarily enough at ground level, look around you as if you were in any cave dwelling—and then begin descending. Kayamakli *goes down fifteen storeys*. We (Vivan and I, Ayesha and Pogey found the tunnels too narrow and the ceilings too low) went down four levels only, marvelling at the ingenuity of these 'builders', thousands of years ago. 'Rooms' were linked by corridors and tunnels that crisscrossed the entire 'floor'.

Each of the fifteen levels had ten 'doors'—massive stone wheels, weighing 300–500 kg each, that were rolled across the openings to prevent entry. Once in place, they could only be operated from the inside. Believe me, you wouldn't want to be caught or trapped on the wrong side of these 'doors'. An ingenious system of smoke signals and mirrors established on the higher levels warned inhabitants of imminent danger—but frankly, we couldn't see anyone attempting to negotiate that labyrinthine maze of tunnels and corridors only to be pulled up short by the 'doors'!

As is to be expected, the more privileged families lived closer to the surface where the air was fresher. They fed on salted meat, dried fruit and nuts. Potatoes store very well in these underground temperatures, and indeed are so stored sometimes, even today. There was provision made for wine coolers, alcoves for candles and other objects, and we saw at least one kitchen—the assumption is that these were communal kitchens, but it could also be that more cold than cooked food was consumed, in order to prevent smoke from being detected.

And just in case you happened to die while in hiding, well, there was room for graves, too.

Primitive and rudimentary these underground cities might have been, but you have to wonder at the ingenuity and skill of those Hittites and everyone who followed, who fashioned for themselves, shelters not dissimilar to air raid bunkers, but with far fewer means at their disposal.

By the time we came back up the rain had stopped, and the sky was that lovely expanse of blue and grey and gold that you get when the sun is shining again, but the rain clouds are still around.

Well, Pogey and I had our Turkish wine on one of Hezen Cave's very nice open terraces, and then we went into Urgüp to eat at Mutti's, a gourmet restaurant that Mehmet at the hotel recommended. It was simply the best meal we had in Turkey. Very subtle fusion, fine ingredients, delicious flavours. The restaurant itself was charming and very tastefully appointed, and Mutti, the owner and master chef, attends to guests himself. Most excellent.

The following morning we took the road less travelled to Mustafapasha, and it was sheer pleasure. Wild poppies and cornflowers, the silence of the ages, rock formations in rose and white, a purple haze of some wild flower (Ayesha bought a book on *Wild Flowers of Turkey* so that we could try and identify it later), soft green grasses. And in the middle of this silence, a revelation, an old family church. Pançarlik. Tenth century, one of Cappadocia's oldest churches. Rough-hewn, like the others, but with beautiful frescoes. They were badly damaged, yes, but the emerald green and wine red were still aglow. One naïvely endearing image of the baby Jesus being bathed depicted him as rather adult, but as such a rendering isn't too common, one can excuse anatomical errors…Somehow, the intimacy of the church, the gentleness of the landscape despite the rocks, and the absence of people made for a rare harmony, and all one's senses responded to it.

We carried that sublime sense of well-being to the Keyselik monastery, another rock-cut one, but set in verdant green, amid old trees. Its remarkable chapel was smoke-charred and quite badly damaged, having been used by villagers to cook in, but we could see that the frescoes were fairly sophisticated. A little church close by had only geometric frescoes, having been painted in the Iconoclastic period.

It was only natural that we end this day of quiet discovery at Zelve, a monastic settlement of monasteries and churches dating to the ninth–thirteenth centuries, and inhabited till as late as 1952. Zelve is as vast and impressive as Göreme, but completely different. More feminine, more in tune with nature, with green hillsides and wild flowers almost crowding out the rocks. The rocks are said to be the most beautiful in Cappadocia, and it may be that the beauty of the surrounding landscape has rubbed off on the large and small, conical and pyramid-shaped fairy chimneys. I don't know. All I know is that walking through Zelve, moving in and out of the churches, stopping to admire the flowers and listen to the birds, was utterly satisfying. Indeed, this whole day had that quality of calm serenity that you experience only rarely on trips like these.

Oh, there was so much more to see in Cappadocia, whole valleys we hadn't been to, the Ihlara canyons being the most important, but our time here was running out and the next morning we had to leave for Izmir and Şirinçe on the south-west coast. Well, Izmir is on the Aegean coast, but Sirinçe is in the hills, up near Ephesus.

THE SOUTH-WEST AND AEGEAN COAST

At the airport the next morning, they told us that no flights had either taken off or landed in Nevşehir the previous day—bad weather. Looked pretty gloomy now, too, but we were assured the plane would take off. We certainly hoped so, we had a connecting flight in Istanbul, where we would also connect with Ratna who was arriving from Delhi.

Şirinçe is one hour away from Izmir, so that by the time we got there and found our way to the Nisanyan Hotel it was quite late in the evening. Still light, though. The Nisanyan is located in a perfectly lovely spot, forested and verdant, flowers and streams, birds, bees, donkeys—and peacocks! But it is a hilly region and our cottages were located up and down fairly steep slopes which had to be negotiated daily—and sometimes more than once or twice—to get anywhere. Gulp.

Well, no pain, no gain, as Aung told us in Myanmar…

Bunny had her own cottage, 'The Hideaway' (which she didn't much like because of creepie-crawlies), with its own garden-plus-hammock and a panoramic view of the hills from a lovely verandah. Ayesha and Vivan were in the 'Indigo Cottage', Jon and Ratna in 'Mon Desir' and Pogey and me in a nice long room in 'The Tower', which had four other rooms and a huge kitchen, where Ferda, the cook, held cooking classes for guests!

Waking up in Şirinçe was heavenly. Smoky blue hills, a light mist, early morning bird calls (including rather loud peacock cries) and the freshest, cleanest air with its fresh, clean fragrance. A piney green fragrance. You could linger over breakfast for hours, because it was served outdoors, overlooking hills and vales, right upto 11 a.m. or noon, if Ferda was feeling generous. Everything was organic, freshly made on the premises from their own produce. Ferda's husband made the honey, for example, and both Jon and Vivan declared it was the best ever. The breads (baked by Ferda) were wonderful, and all the cheeses—in olive oil with herbs, or by themselves—were delicious. As was the watermelon, the peaches, the strawberries. And every morning, there would be a different, divine cake that Ferda had baked. Walnut. Coffee. Carrot and ginger…

Nisanyan is family-owned, the first of the boutique hotels in the region (some say in the country), started by a husband-and-wife team who came to Şirinçe as students over thirty-five years ago—and stayed. They started with converting three village houses into cottages and now have eight, set in twenty acres of landscaped hillside, wild grasses, herb gardens and flowers. And olive trees, which yield quantities of oil used in all their cooking.

Obviously a favourite with Americans looking for a different kind of luxury, one that entails some rusticity as well! So, if you want to dine at the hotel, you have to order well in advance because food is cooked in specific quantities, and the desserts, especially, are made while you're eating. Makes for a very nice experience, indeed. The chocolate soufflé and fruit strudel were superb.

We decided to explore the old village of Şirinçe in the morning, located downhill from the Nisanyan. Quite a steep walk down from the hotel, through little streets and villagers' homes, to emerge on the village square which was quite lovely. Shops, of course, always such a pleasure to walk along aisles of them, selling dried fruit (apricots and figs are just the best), spices, herbs, exotic teas (apple, jasmine, mint, chamomile, peach, lavender and many combinations thereof), cheeses, olives and olive products— oils, soaps, creams—jewellery and clothes, crafts, textiles, toys, junk, all sorts of stuff.

Right on the square was an old-fashioned coffee place—open seating under an awning, rough tables and chairs, a brazier for Turkish coffee. But a brazier with hot gravel, not coals. This called for a coffee break. The owner picked up one of these long-handled little vessels, spooned in coffee and sugar, added water and set it down in the gravel. Then went to get us our (weak) filter coffees. The little vessel bubbled and bubbled, then almost bubbled over, when it was snatched up and the thick dark liquid poured into glasses. Mid-morning was clearly a time when local villagers, men and women, paused for coffee and catching up.

Sonia, at Nisanyan, told us that the two churches in the village were worth seeing, so we wound our way towards one of them, the bigger one, but were waylaid by the jewellery shop. Stopped just to look, but stayed for almost half an hour because Ayesha found earrings and a bangle that she wanted. This entailed some very smooth sales talk on the part of the sales girl and boy, and some polite but determined bargaining on Ayesha's. Turkish jewellery design is definitely different—silver and gemstones as in India, but much more imaginative and artistic. Also very well made. Ayesha's patience paid off, and she was what she calls 'a happy bunny' at the end of the exchange!

Şirinçe village has the same charm as many Italian and French small towns—hilly with winding streets full of shops and eateries, all enticing. We encountered many of these, stopping frequently to look, bargain, buy, and finally arrived at our church, only to find that it was under restoration. Never ones to be deterred by this minor detail, we peeked in (the door was open) and were at least able to admire its proportions and see that it was clearly Greek Orthodox.

Meanwhile, I was still on the lookout for a wine shop to buy some local wine, and was told to go to the shop down the road from the church, to the right. Okay. But this was a clothes shop, with a few bottles of wine in a corner. The cellar, however, was down a steep ladder and it had a huge selection. I tasted at least four different reds, then bought one which was a blend of two Turkish grapes, bottled by a German vintner. And very good it was. Even Ratna agreed.

We then ate what was possibly our best lunch in Şirinçe, in a little Greek restaurant, totally deserted when we got there. Not a good sign, we thought, but then the owner and his wife showed up and made everything right there, fresh and delicious. The salad, the bôrek, Vivan's beef dish with aubergines, Pogey's lamb with veggies…True to its promise outside:

> This mansion left from a Greek family is 250 years old and the owners are living here since 1924, after the population exchange, cooking local food for you and sharing the mansion for accommodation.
>
> If your reason to come here is seeing history of the place, we await you…
>
> If you are in a rush, you can just have a drink in the beautiful garden behind the mansion.

After lunch and on the spur of the moment we decided to go to Ephesus (Efes in Turkish, Apasa in Hittite)—after all, it was only 20–30 km away. Maybe less. We'd seen it earlier, Pogey and I, in 1998–99, but one can see ruins again and again, can't one? We'd been advised to avoid early mornings and late afternoons at Ephesus, which is when the cruise ships disgorge their hordes, so we were there during the hottest part of the day. All that white marble blazing away in the midday sun.

There are probably more Greek ruins in Turkey than there are in Greece, and Ephesus is certainly among the most spectacular. Temples. Processional streets. Terraced houses. Toilets. Baths. The original proscenium theatre, still built today as it was then. Very sophisticated sculpture. And a library building that is rivalled only by the one across the Mediterranean in Alexandria. We ogled and admired, tried to take it all in, tried to avoid the tourists who seemed more interested in taking selfies, but the thing about ruins like Ephesus (as, for instance in Egypt, with Karnak) is that they are simply overwhelming. Statements, as Ayesha remarked—in 18 pt. Caps, if you know what I mean.

As we walked down its streets and rubber-necked our way towards the library and theatre, I tried frantically to recall its history—built in the tenth century BC; under the Romans in the first century BC; the third largest city in Asia Minor—while excitedly sighting the statues of Hermes and Nike, winged goddess of victory. And then, in front of Hadrian's Temple, trying hard to conjure up the statuary and fountains shown in the sketch alongside the ruin, but not really succeeding. One picture may be worth a thousand words, but it doesn't stand a chance in front of the real thing.

Where one *could* imagine the action was in the Odeon amphitheatre, a magnificent example, seating up to 6,000 spectators. Perfect proportions, perfect acoustics.

Pogey climbed up to the highest tier of seats and spoke, conversationally, to Vivan who had just entered below, and every word was as clear as a bell. Yes, one could well imagine *Electra* and *Oedipus* and all the Greek tragedies in performance here, under an open sky, lit by flares.

For the famous Temple of Artemis, however, we would have to wait till we went to the Ephesus Museum in Selçuk, because the temple was destroyed by a Christian mob in 400 AD. Only one of its famed 127 columns is now standing, and the town itself was partially levelled by an earthquake in 614 AD. We're horrified today by the vandalising of the Bamiyan Buddhas and the landmining of Palmyra—and so we should be—but forget that pillage and plunder and ransacking were the norm for victorious armies. Almost all places of worship, pagan or other, were destroyed by those who came later and venerated other gods.

The world is full of such ruins, and the world's museums full of stolen sculptures.

On the way back to Nisanyan and Şirinçe, I couldn't help thinking of what we had seen in Cappadocia, roughly the same period as Ephesus, with more or less the same span of centuries, and wondering at the primitiveness of the cave churches and dwellings. Was there no contact at all, then, between Central and Ionian Turkey? Yet, if the excavations at Sobessos in Cappa are any indication, then the Romans were building there very early on, and not building underground cities or temples in caves, either. A riddle.

Saturday is market day in Selçuk and so off we went to the market, to be followed by a visit to the Ephesus Museum, just across the way from it. As is common across Europe, weekly markets sell everything from needles to camels (well, almost), and as always, the fruit and vegetable stalls are the most seductive. How to resist those luscious cherries and peaches? Those delectable apricots? We didn't. Good thing, too, because they were demolished on the way to Pirene that afternoon! So were the pistas, hazelnuts and peanuts that practically spilled over into our hands and had themselves bought.

Most of the treasures excavated at Ephesus are in the museum at Selçuk. Begun in 1873 by the British, excavations were continued till the end of the century, financed by the Germans and Australians, the latter active till today. (In fact, the Australian Archaeological Institute is responsible for much excavation activity on other Turkish sites as well.)

The Selçuk sculptures are splendid. Here, in this contained space, artfully lit and displayed, you are up close (but not personal), close enough to appreciate the tremendous skill, as well as the power and beauty, of these gods and heroes. The massive head of Domitian reminded me of the fallen statue in Sicily—not Icarus, but the enormous one at Segesta, I think it was, lying on its side, decapitated. But it was the two Artemises in the museum that had me mesmerised. In a room by themselves, spotlit, facing each other. Artemis the Huntress, hung with all her trophies—bulls' testicles, lion heads, all that she had slain she wore as her raiment, covered from neck to ankles with these medals. Visually breathtaking, and a most unusual representation, for no other gods were similarly hung with their attributes. Visible her attributes may have been, but to look at her face was to look into the unknowable.

Ratna, who was determined to see 'every single Greek and Roman ruin in the region', said we should now go to Aphrodisias, Pergamum, Priene and Miletus, as well as Didyma. Why? we asked, why do we need to see them all? Because. After some amount of back and forth and some sound advice from our driver, Shakir, regarding distances, and so on, we decided we'd go to Priene and Miletus, close to each other, and save Aphrodisias for later.

Priene and Miletus, two Greek towns, are what Pogey said were 'grid-iron settlements' on promontories—a complete no-no in town planning. But the original Priene, the oldest city, was a port city at the mouth of the Menderes river, which had to be abandoned as the river kept silting up, turning the city into a marshy swamp. In the fourth century BC, the Persians moved it up to its present location but it remained small, its population never exceeding 3,000–4,000.

There was almost no one at Priene when we got there, and we discovered why. A *very* steep climb up to the top, a settlement almost completely in ruin. Huge remnants of columns and boulders strewn across the site, barely recognisable structures, tall trees and grasses obscuring what was left of a council chamber—it was beautiful. So quiet, so returned to itself. Here, it was so much easier to transport oneself back several centuries, imagine worshippers at the Temple of Athena—only a little smaller than the Artemis Temple at Ephesus, with 122 columns. This one still had five standing. Abandonment apart, Priene is supposed to be the one Greek city which is more or less intact, albeit in ruins. With almost no tourists around we wandered as if it was there just for us, strayed into the smaller of the two theatres, still well preserved and with VIP chairs in front—the only ones I've ever seen in a theatre—allowing the desolation of the place to seep in. It's not a bad feeling at all, in fact quite welcome, this respite from noise and speed. It wasn't only the climb up that slowed us down, Priene imposed its own slow pace. Actually allowed us to empty our minds of the riches in the Ephesus Museum in order to take this desolation in.

Vivan, who had been looking up places to eat at in *Lonely Planet* said the best place to do so was close by, but when we asked a passerby for directions she informed us that it had closed down three years ago! She sent us to another restaurant, though, where we had the lightest, most delicate pancake ever, called gözleme. Wafer-thin, with spinach and cheese, made in front of our eyes on an enormous griddle, by the owner's wife. Cut up into bite-sized pieces and served with salad. Spot on.

Post this late lunch we voted to skip Miletus and Didyma (much to Ratna's disgust), especially if they entailed the kind of climb we had just done. Pogey thought the two would be very similar to Priene, and so we wended our way back to Selçuk and Şirinçe, well pleased with the day's discoveries.

Should we go to Aphrodisias the following day or take it easy, it being Sunday, and we being in need of a bit of rest? Pros and cons of putting off what would be a long trip on the day before another journey (to Istanbul) were weighed, and we agreed to spend the day at Nisanyan, enjoying the environment. It turned out to be a beautiful, peaceful day, spent on the breakfast terrace, reading and writing, walking a bit, eating a lunch of bread and cheese and fruit, then going down to the village for dinner and a stroll. Walking in Şirinçe was always an unhurried experience, with an occasional surprise around the corner in the form of a shop dealing only in felt goods, or an antique shop full of objects from Central Asia…or an outdoor restaurant and garden from where you could see the sun go down on the hill across the valley. Over a glass of wine, naturally.

Tried to leave as early as possible for Aphrosidias the next day as it is a good 160 km from Selçuk, but it was close to 10.30 a.m. by the time we left Selçuk.

Aphrodisias is definitely a feminine site, just as Ephesus is clearly masculine. Ayesha and I were agreed on this. We felt it as soon as we reached the entrance, even before we saw the magnificent Tetrapylon, the monumental gateway to the Temple of Aphrodite. It was a combination of things—the most beautiful ruin in Turkey was set in nature, a part of it, not sculpted out of or dominating it. There was green all around, the columns and arches and other remains scattered across the landscape, a subtle harmony suffusing the atmosphere. Here, too, there were few tourists, and an overcast sky lent a soft outline to the entire site.

Excavations at Aphrodisias proved that the acropolis here was a prehistoric mound, built up successively by various rulers from about 5000 BC on. By the third century BC, it had become the capital of a Roman province, with a population of 15,000. Under the Byzantines, the temple was converted into a Christian church, and the town continued as a cathedral town well into the middle ages. It was abandoned in the twelfth century—who knows why? And then an earthquake destroyed it in 1956.

That stunning Tetrapylon was rebuilt by anastylosis after major excavations were undertaken by Professor Kennan T. Erin, a Turkish archaeologist at New York University. He directed the excavations from 1961 till 1991, and is buried at the site.

I'm so glad we went to Aphrodisias after Ephesus. Experienced it in all its understated beauty, felt its quiet perfection as we moved from ruined temple to agora to theatre to Hadrian's Bath—and then to the stadium. We gasped in amazement. The only fully preserved ancient stadium extant, a perfect oval, 270 metres long, with seating for 30,000. It was a sight to behold, supreme in itself and in its grandeur. Today's stadia seem so puny by comparison. A gentle rain accompanied us on our walk in Aphrodisias, almost like a benediction. I was glad, too, that Aphrodisias was our last ruin, because any other would have been anticlimactic.

We thought we had seen quite fantastic sculptures in the Ephesus Museum, but what we found in the museum at Aphrodisias was far richer and more extensive.

Whole panels and friezes, individual figures, hundreds of them, room after room of heroic and mythic tales, gods, goddesses, warriors, kings and nobles, noblewomen and slaves…an endless bounty. Our senses reeled.

* * *

Istanbul. Constantinople. Byzantium. So many layers, associations, histories of conquest and assimilation, of overlapping traditions, colliding faiths, conflicting politics…

On 7 June voting took place in Turkey, in a keenly contested and tense election, but campaigning had been rather low-key—by Indian standards at any rate. True, we had been far from the madding crowd for most of the time, but still. By the time we reached Istanbul on 9 June the results had been declared, and Muge Sokmen (of the publishing house, Metis, and our host for the meeting of the English Language Network of the International Alliance of Independent Publishers) was jubilant. Tayyip Erdogan had failed to get a majority, and the Kurdish National Party had managed to get more than 10 per cent of the votes, which meant they were now a national party. But this fractured vote also meant uncertainty—Erdogan dismissed the possibility of a coalition government, and other parties would probably not have the numbers to form one without them. An old, old predicament here in India, but a new and troubling one for Turkey.

Pogey's birthday on 9 June, and his birthday dinner had been planned weeks earlier by Bunny and Ratna—

we would go to Muzedechang, a restaurant highly recommended by one and all. We had no idea what we were letting ourselves in for, but having made a booking already from Cappadocia, off we went.

Well, Muzedechang was miles away from where we were staying, just off Taksim Square, and it took us a good one hour to get there. Once we arrived, however, we understood why it's so special. The restaurant is part of a private museum, set on a hill overlooking the Bosphorus, amid trees and gardens; we sat on the terrace from where we could see all the way across the river to the other shore, with cruise ships plying on the water.

The museum belongs to one of Turkey's richest families, originally in the cotton business (having appropriated huge tracts of cotton-growing farmland from Kurds in southeastern Turkey), but now concentrating on electronics and hi-tech communication. Houri, Ayesha's friend, an economist, who joined us for dinner, said the museum had a very good collection of medieval calligraphy, and organised special exhibitions of contemporary European and Turkish art.

The food was wonderful, all of it—starters, mains, desserts, but I passed up the octopus and calamari! Sitting out on a balmy evening, with good wine and food, Houri regaling us with local gossip (including her University of Chicago friendship with Ahmed Chalabi as a young PhD student, later meeting him when he became de facto advisor on Iraq to the US State Department…); her opinions on everything from the election results (pro-

Erdogan) to Orhan Pamuk's Museum of Innocence (self-indulgent)—we agreed that we had chosen well.

Houri's opinion notwithstanding, we decided that we should see the Museum of Innocence anyway, as it is the only museum in the world based on a book. As a publisher, how could I not visit it? Well, getting to it turned out to be not quite as simple as we had been told ('Oh, it's just fifteen minutes from your hotel,' Muge said) and, as we discovered, was the case with most directions in Istanbul. We walked and walked and walked, and finally after a good forty-five minutes or more, arrived at a tall, narrow building on a lovely, winding street called Çukurçuma. This was it.

Self-indulgent it certainly is, but it is also one of the most interesting museums I have visited. Based on Pamuk's novel of the same name, it recounts the life of Kemal Basmaci, who used to live in the building. Set in the period 1974–2000, it recreates the life and times of two Istanbul families, one wealthy, the other middle class. Kemal, wealthy, is set to marry Sibel, a girl from his social class, when he falls in love with Füsun, a distant relative, who works as a sales assistant in a shop. They meet clandestinely, and after Füsun marries someone else, Kemal visits her in this building, now a museum. After each visit, he takes back one object that reminds him of Füsun, as a memento. It is these objects that form the core collection of the museum.

The exhibits are displayed on four floors, in seventy glass-fronted, rectangular cabinets or vitrines on the walls, each unit containing an eclectic, often unrelated, set of objects—photographs, newspaper clippings, memorabilia—illustrating one chapter of the book. The assumption is that disparate objects, used for different purposes and evocative of the most random memories can, when placed alongside each other, bring forth unexpected emotions and responses. An intriguing and seductive proposition, and a fascinating curatorial exercise. Each cabinet carries a corresponding chapter title from the book, and the whole exhibition is so designed as to present an experience of Istanbul society, mid-century, while at the same time, 'fictionalising' it by making Kemal's life and love its central focus. We found it both provocative and, as Pogey said, palpably authentic.

There is just one 'exhibit' on the fourth floor, Kemal's bedroom, where he lived from 2000 to 2007, and where Pamuk interviewed him for his book. Because you visit this floor last, after 'reading' the rest of the museum, you register keenly the poignancy and pathos of Kemal's doomed love.

Pamuk's book and the museum have both come in for a fair bit of criticism by writers and intellectuals in Turkey, probably with good reason, but it's hard to quarrel with his motivation or with his concept of what a museum should be. Before or after you 'see' the book as an exhibition, Pamuk sets out his criteria for what he thinks a museum should be. In his 'A Manifesto for Museums' he says

> Small museums in the back streets of European cities led me to realise that museums—just like novels—can speak for individuals. That is not to understate the importance of the Met or Topkapi or Prado or Louvre…

>...But I am against these precious monumental institutions being used as blueprints for future museums. Museums should explore and uncover the universe and humanity of the new and modern man emerging from increasingly wealthy non-Western nations...

I have to say I agree with most of his sentiments (modern man apart), and to the extent that he has attempted a radical reconsideration of what constitutes an 'exhibit', the museum is commendable.

Many of us remember Pamuk for having been indicted by the government for writing about the genocide of the Kurds. He became a cause célèbre (some say it also ensured he was awarded the Nobel), and for others, his celebrity distracted from the real and ever-present censorship that prevails in Turkey. Muge organised a meeting for us with the Publishers' Association of Turkey, during which we heard, first-hand, from those indomitable and courageous publishers who had been taken to court, times without number; been convicted and imprisoned on charges of defamation; been hounded and threatened—but had stood firm.

According to a report put out by the Turkish Publishers' Association, covering the period June 2014–June 2015, there has been an alarming increase in attempts to censor by instituting investigations against offending journals and publishers. Any opinion that is critical of or opposes the views and positions of the politically powerful in the country, is perceived as an 'insult' or, worse, as 'defamatory'. Political dissent is subjected to intimidation, and a huge number of lawsuits by the government, against newspapers, articles in books or in periodicals, have resulted in substantial fines being imposed, as well as in prison terms for writers, cartoonists, artists and publishers.

One stark example of this was the case of the book, *Ghezi Phenomenon*, published by Idea Politika, after the protests in Taksim Square in 2013. Erol Ozkoray, the author, was charged with 'insulting' the prime minister, Tayyip Erdogan, and in September 2014 he was sentenced to eleven months and twenty days in prison. Although the court 'postponed' announcing the verdict for five years, he is still charged.

Similarly, the daily newspaper, *Çumhuriyet*, decided to publish a selection of the *Charlie Hebdo* cartoons, including a depiction of the Prophet, on its cover. The police raided the printing press after midnight (without a judge's order) searched the delivery trucks, and stopped distribution of the newspaper. Two columnists were put on trial for publishing the visual of the Prophet in their columns, and currently, the paper's journalists are charged with forty-one criminal cases, are facing sixteen criminal investigations, and have thirty-three monetary compensation suits pending against them.

Muge herself, and Metis, have been taken to court many times and, though acquitted, have had to suffer the harassment each time, including during the Gezi Park resistance.

I used to think that Egypt's censorship laws were probably the most draconian in the region, but Turkey seems to be as repressive, with or without an actual law. In 2014, Turkey was ranked the third most prohibitive country in the world for its social media censorship.

Istanbul is testimony to the impression that Turkey is the Orient in the Occident and the Occident in the Orient, for nowhere (in my experience) is this meeting of cultures so evident—and so richly present. In its architecture, its history, its art, its people. Even its language, a blend of Hungarian, French and Persian, is rather unique. It is impossible to step into any of its churches or mosques without being made immediately aware of their layered history, not just of observance, but of tolerance. Can one spend even ten minutes in Hagia Sophia without being moved and humbled by its soaring architecture and the imagination (and skill) that conceptualised it, but also by the fact that Greeks, Christians and Turks all respected its sanctity, regardless of religious belief? Its ultimate secularisation in 1935, by Kemal Ataturk, was its almost inevitable twentieth-century avatar as a museum.

And just as there are almost more Greek and Roman ruins in Turkey than in Greece or Rome, so too, the mosaics in Hagia Sophia, the Kayeri Church, and indeed in the Great Mosaic Museum, are as splendid and sophisticated as any in Italy or Sicily.

The Bosphorus separates the Asian side of Istanbul from the European, and if you look across the river from the European side to the Asian, the skyscape is punctuated by minarets, like so many exclamation marks in the sky. And when you walk the streets of Sultanahmet, you might easily think you're in the Medina in Fez or Rabat or Marrakesh…

Muge, bless her soul, organised a cruise on a private boat down the Bosphorus for us, which was wonderful. We were fifteen, and the boat was the last word in comfort—one might almost say luxury. Fitted with a dining table, deep armchairs and sofas on the upper deck, three people serving us food and wine (or whisky, beer, gin, vodka), sailing north towards the point where the river meets the Black Sea. All along the coast was evidence of the incredible building activity, eclectic and eccentric, that had taken place in Istanbul during the previous two centuries. Semih, Muge's husband, gave us a snapshot history of many of the palaces and mansions along the shore (including one used by the Germans in World War I, and another where Semih was temporarily imprisoned for being AWOL while in military service!), more proof of the great wealth of the Ottoman Empire. Like London or Paris, Istanbul too, was supported by the colonies, a fact we tend to forgot. And like London or Paris, it is a supremely urban and cosmopolitan city. It's hard to imagine, walking down the heaving, pulsating Istiklal Street at 2 a.m., that Erdogan's government is trying to infuse an Islamic flavour into the country, even though we did see more veiled women in Istanbul than in Selçuk or Cappadocia. Of course, they could have been tourists from elsewhere.

On our last night in the city, Indu, Antoinette, Jed and I decided to go to a hookah café around the corner from our hotel, and it was a most fitting and satisfying conclusion to the entire trip!

The Citadel of Aleppo (above), and (below) The Ruins at Baalbek

Lebanon and Syria: The Lure of the Levant

April–May 2009

The Levant, the Holy Land, lure to the Phoenicians and Romans and Greeks and, later, the Arabs and Turks, now the cradle of conflict with all the tensions and irresolutions converging on Lebanon and Syria—how was it possible not to want to see and experience this for ourselves, if only fleetingly, briefly, a region that beckoned from far away and so very long ago?

You arrive in Beirut and you know immediately that—unlike say, Istanbul in Turkey—you are definitely not in Europe even though you are on the Mediterranean. It's not just the urban landscape that's different, not just the many dilapidated or abandoned or even bullet-ridden and bombed-out buildings that you notice more often than you'd expect, it's that it is proudly and clearly Arab. Despite road names and signs in French, English and Arabic, despite blond hair and blue eyes, it is Arab—and very cosmopolitan. Everyone remarks on the indefinable and special urbanity and poise of the Beiruti, and there seems to be something to that. We weren't in the city long enough to find out for ourselves, but then we sort of had an 'inside' view through Hasna Mekdashi and her family. Hasna, apart from being a founder of the only feminist press in the Arab world, Nour, also organised a pioneering Arab Women Writers' Book Fair in Cairo in the mid-1990s.

I reached Beirut after an interrupted overnight flight from London. Hasna met me at the airport and took me to her daughter Rana's apartment where we would be staying, as Rana was in Cairo (in Hasna and her husband Muhammad's flat there) for the rest of the month. After a most welcome cup of tea and a shower, Hasna returned and took me to lunch to a very pleasant restaurant in the centre of town, generally known as Solidere, after the company that financed and oversaw the reconstruction of downtown Beirut following the fifteen-year civil war. We walked through the pedestrianised streets, looking at what Pogey refers to as the 'fake historicity' of a reconstructed past through colonial look-alike buildings. Very elegant, at one level, exorbitantly expensive, and a perfect example of profit-driven development. As became increasingly clear from Hasna's account of whose brainchild this project was—ex-President Rafik Hariri's, killed when a car bomb exploded in May 2005—and who benefited from it. Bankers, primarily, Hariri and family, and a few canny investors who paid modest compensations for buying prime real estate (approximately 200 buildings from the Ottoman and French Mandate periods, costing billions of dollars). In 2006, Hassan Nasrallah's Hezbollah occupied the Beirut Central District, setting up a tented camp in its core area.

Later that evening at Hasna's place for dinner, Muhammad disagreed with her analysis, saying that Solidere was owned by 'at least 10,000 individuals', so Hariri couldn't be blamed for all the ills of the Beirut Central District. There followed a spirited exchange between them on the pros and cons of such 'ownership', till finally they agreed to disagree. All this over a delicious dinner cooked by Muhammad—a most delicate fish in lemon sauce and herbs; cracked wheat and lentils; cracked wheat and tomatoes; olives and cheese; a huge salad; beetroots, and Lebanese wine. Ksara? Not sure, but probably.

Byblos, we thought, would be a good way to spend Sunday, a spot of ancient Rome, a fish lunch at one of its harbour restaurants, then on to Tripoli, to see its famous Khan Sabon or Souk of Soaps, Tripoli being well known for its soap. North Lebanon today, South on Monday, and Baalbek in East Lebanon on Tuesday, was the plan. It's such a small narrow country that doing all three directions seemed completely manageable. Not like Syria, which is vast. A very pleasant drive along the coast, and we were in Byblos in an hour or so. A charming seaside town, hilly, hugging a bay with the Roman ruins beautifully sited on a high outcrop. A perfect setting for a jewel-like amphitheatre, the smallest I've ever seen, with the sea as a backdrop. Actually, the most dramatic of these theatres would have been the one at Tyre—reputed to hold 20,000 spectators; who would have thought there were so many inhabitants in that small town?—but being completely destroyed now, we could only imagine its impact. The one at Byblos is perfectly preserved, though relocated, Pogey says. What enchanted me most at Byblos was the wildness of the ruin, the scattered remains visible through clusters of bright red poppies and grass daisies and a brilliant yellow flower whose name escapes me.

We should have lingered and had lunch at one of its seashore restaurants, but thought we might just as well do that at Tripoli, where we were told there were equally good fish places. That was a mistake. We never did find a good restaurant, and Tripoli was disappointing. A bit tumble-down, almost shabby, even though it is Lebanon's second-largest city. And the souk was closed, it being Sunday, so the whole point of going there was defeated. Ah, well...the drive there gave us an opportunity to see the countryside, although you could hardly call it that, it was one continuous habitation.

Dinner that evening at Hasna's was wholly memorable, not just for the food—kibbeh, raw and grilled (for me), lasagna (for Mourid), a great big salad (primarily for Hasna who'd been asked to watch her diet for BP, diabetes and cholesterol), and of course, the usual Lebanese savouries of tabouleh, olives and cheese. Plus the red wine I had brought from London.

I was meeting Mourid after twelve years, having first met him with Radwa in Cairo in 1997. An amazing man and mind, what the Tamils would call 'a r-ayar individual', a wonderful poet and terrific raconteur. Also a clown, as Hasna said fondly. In exile from Palestine for thirty-three or more years, since 1967 actually, then in Budapest for almost twenty years representing the Palestine Liberation Organisation (PLO)—the Egyptians wouldn't allow him to live in Egypt, though he's married to an Egyptian, because of his PLO links—later in disfavour with the PLO because he didn't agree with various compromises they made, so he eventually became a full-time writer and poet. *I Saw Ramallah*, his lyrical and deeply moving account of returning to Palestine after thirty-three years, is one of the most powerful testimonies I have read on exile, a work that haunts and disturbs you each time you return to it. Mourid, who has written:

> *I rubbed the leaf of the orange in my hands*
> *As I had been told to do*
> *So that I could smell its scent*
> *But before my hand could reach my nose*
> *I had lost my home and become a refugee*

That evening Mourid was, in turn, bitter and passionate about Palestine, about how the craven politics of the UK and US had systematically destroyed every secular, political option in the Middle East for over sixty years, beginning with 1947 and the creation of Israel, followed by the overthrow of Prime Minister Mohammad Mossadegh in Iran, right up to all their misadventures in this century. Iran, Iraq, Syria, Lebanon, Jordan, Egypt, Israel, Palestine—one long history of meddlesome and disastrous politicking, leaving a region scarred and devastated by years and years of violence. And the Muslim Brotherhood in

Egypt, masquerading as moderates—'The moderates are the real hell,' he said, 'because they provide no opposition and no alternative'—left him full of a kind of ferocious despair for that country and their life in it.

And so he retreats into his poetry, which is never bitter, but always compelling and compassionate, a sustained and philosophical reflection on loss and separation.

I was so happy to have met him again.

Decided, after discussing with Hasna, that we would hire a taxi for the day and go south, to Tyre (now Sour), Sidon (Saida) and stop at the seventeenth-century Ottoman Palace of Emir Bachir Chahabi at Beit-ed Dine on the way. So we set off with Jamal, an ex-employee of Muhammad's, general dogsbody, who now runs a taxi service ('Wallah, I take peoples from Amnesty, UN, all good people, very nice,') and who kept up a running commentary on every village and town we passed. 'Here, Druze and Massihi,' he would say, meaning Christian and a Shiite sect found mostly in Lebanon, 'here Hezbollah,' as we drove further south into Lebanon's poorer region. With fourteen seats in Parliament, Hezbollah is an important political party, but more than that, a provider of basic services like schools and clinics and employment to the poor who have been treated to Beirut's indifference for a very long time.

Lebanon is the only country in the world whose polity is categorised and represented along religious lines: Christian, Shia, Sunni, Druze, and a strict balance is preserved as far as representation goes. Although majority Muslim (40 per cent Christian currently), power has always been in the hands of the Maronite Christians, and local and national politics have always been divisive. So much so, that the 1975–76 civil war between Christians and Muslims saw them physically separated in Beirut by the infamous Green Line: Christians to the west, Muslims in the east. That line no longer exists but the tensions simmer, very close to the surface.

Well, Beit-ed Dine was closed, continuing our run of mistimed visits. Monday. But none of the guide books said so, mentioning only winter and summer timings. We saw it from the outside, a beautifully elegant palace perched high on a mountain, holding out real promise for what to expect inside. We'd have to see if we had time to return.

It being nearly noon by now, we decided to skip Sidon and go straight to Tyre, another coastal town, an ancient Roman city famous for the ruins still being excavated. A World Heritage Site, like much else in Lebanon. But first, lunch. We found a charming small restaurant, Le Petit Phoenician, run by a former midshipman who had roamed the world on an oil tanker. 'India?' he said, 'I have been to Colombo,' thinking it's one and the same, isn't it?! We both had his fish, Pogey's fresh, mine frozen, his good, mine not, but my orange juice was freshly squeezed and delicious.

Post-lunch we walked through its tiny streets to reach the promenade by the marina, which was truly beautiful. A wide curve of sea, very few people, a wonderful vista—and dangerously close to Israel. How often had they arrived by sea and bombed the area around the city because this is Hezbollah country. Indeed, till very recently, the countryside was still supposed to be landmined, and Lebanese soldiers and artillery line the route all the way down. You are stopped at every check-post, the suspicion being that Israeli spies frequently sneak in to gather intelligence.

Tyre is splendid. As you enter the site, you see this row of columns, still standing, on either side of what was the agora, flanked by residential quarters and Roman baths. Brick-vaulted, well-preserved, so that one can imagine their form and scale. It's a huge complex, must have been quite a citadel, and as you approach the second row of double colonnaded columns that line a mosaic street, you get some idea of the conceptualisation. The street would have culminated in an enormous theatre, nothing of which now remains, unfortunately, but can you just see those performances, gladiatorial fights or jousting, with the Mediterranean gleaming in the background? A vast theatrical panorama of sea and sky, an audience of thousands, a spectacle worth witnessing, if only one could.

As we neared Beirut on the way back, I thought why not make a short detour and see Sabra and Shatila, the Palestinian refugee camps in which the Phalangist massacres of 1976 took place, killing mainly women and children. Sabra and Shatila have become metaphors for the plight of the Palestinian displaced, but they are also the place where 12–13,000 people now live, of whom according to Hasna, only about 5,000 are Palestinian. The rest are made up of all the poor in Lebanon—Bangladeshis, poor Lebanese, poor Iranis and Syrians, fugitives of one kind or another.

The site of the massacre is a kind of enclosed green space full of overgrown grass and weeds, with huge blow-ups of those killed on tottering stands, some torn and fluttering forlornly in the breeze. It's sad and shocking at the same time, not just this memorial but the whole area, desperately poor, the 'camps' actually tenements, the streets full of kiosks selling cheap wares, fruit and vegetable carts, junk shops, people milling around, an atmosphere of great decrepitude and hopelessness.

Palestinians in Lebanon are the nowhere people—no rights, no jobs (by law they cannot be employed in over seventy types of jobs including all the professions, government service and most of the formal sector), no prospect of betterment through commerce, not allowed to buy land, so condemned to subsistence living and illegal livelihood. And no government or political party could be bothered because they don't want them around anyway. Except for the Hezbollah who want justice for the Sabra and Shatila massacres, the Palestinians are best forgotten. While the PLO was still active, it looked after the educational and health needs of the refugees, found employment for them, gave them dignity and reason to hope; but with its decline and sidelining by the Palestinian Authority, the refugees are no one's responsibility.

Bad as they are, Sabra and Shatila are nowhere near as horrific as the camp near the airport where, according to Hasna, there are 30–40,000 refugees, living in abysmal, inhuman conditions.

What a blot on the world's conscience, but mostly, and most reprehensibly, on Israel's.

Better-off, usually Christian, Palestinians have gone abroad, others who can, make their way to Jordan, Egypt or Syria—which last is the most hospitable to them. Syria grants citizenship, allows them to buy property, educates them. In Lebanon, by contrast, no Palestinian child can go to a public school; if they want to, they have to apply for permission to do so, then pay expensive fees. It's the same in Egypt; Mourid and Radwa's son, Tamim, has Jordanian and Palestinian citizenship even though his mother is Egyptian, so he had to get special concessions to attend a public school in Cairo.

Under the circumstances, it looks like India does a more humane job with her refugees, even though that's not saying much.

Decided to take another crack at Beit-ed Dine, and it was well worth the ride. The palace itself is resplendent Ottoman, all painted woodwork, ceilings, panelling, doors, variegated marble, intricately carved stone and the obligatory Damascene mosaic, more like parquetry with mother-of-pearl inlay. Must say, it didn't really appeal to me. A series of three very gracious courtyards, a hammam of truly interesting features, including ingenious natural lighting, and stables with vaulted stone ceilings of beautiful proportions. Five hundred horses were reportedly stabled here, but now they display some lovely mosaics from the medieval period. Very large, delicately coloured stone in pale brown, rose, black and white, most of them were part of a church at Jiyyeh, near Sidon, the ancient city of Porphyrion, and were discovered in 1982. Byzantine, but not as brilliant or as artful as the ones in Istanbul or Ravenna. Still, definitely worth seeing, and now the pride of Beit-ed Dine, lovingly restored to former glory by Walid Jumblatt, the local Druze governor, and protected from the ravages of the civil war.

An air of great tranquillity pervades the entire complex, the open grassed courtyards affording some lovely views and providing a setting for some of the room-sized mosaics displayed on the grass. Quite unusual. Very few tourists, which added to the feeling of timelessness. Nice.

The following day was dedicated to Baalbek (ancient Heliopolis) 90 km south-east of Beirut, in the Bekaa Valley, a stronghold of the Hezbollah, and just 35 km from the Syrian border. Also the site of the most magnificent ruins we have seen so far. The drive there took us through some real Lebanese countryside, mountain ranges and valleys, and the Bekaa itself is called a valley but is actually a plateau. The oldest wine-producing area in the whole region, it is the home of Lebanon's premier label, Ksara, mostly Cabernet Sauvignon and Syrrah. The Reserve is quite good.

But the whole place is still scarred from the Israeli bombings of 2006, whole hillsides burnt, bridges blown up, buildings destroyed. Every time we passed one such, Jamal would say, 'Here, Israelis bomb, bomb. Coming by sea, and bomb, bomb.' Bounded by Syria, Jordan, Palestine and Israel, Lebanon's location leaves it vulnerable to all, secured from none. Indeed, what Mourid writes about Palestine:

> *War itself,*
> *leaning on its cane*
> *strolls occasionally*
> *down the corridor of peace*

could, unhappily, be as true for Lebanon, albeit not nearly as tragically as for Palestine.

By contrast, Roman conquests almost seem cleaner and more straightforward, no equivocation there, no pretence at self-defence, just out-and-out war and invasion. With spectacular victory monuments and memorials, and towering temples to their gods. How petty and vainglorious contemporary buildings seem by comparison, meagre in conception and scale. At Baalbek, the full glory of the monumentality of both scale and conception are on view, even though the remains are just ruins now. You enter the complex through this massive gate, huge pillars topped by an elaborately carved pediment, into a hexagonal, covered space, the only one extant among all Roman structures. The size of the stones is simply staggering, and drawings of how they were transported over the hills by teams of slaves is an indication of the enormity of the building activity, and of the hundreds who doubtless perished on the job. Into the large rectangular court which held the Great Altar to Jupiter, surrounded by double-columned corridors filled with statuary, domed and carved, and in the end, an expanse of steps leading up to the sanctum, quite destroyed now, but the columns and pillars and enormous stones that still stand, speak volumes. All you can do is stand and stare. And look upon it with wonder and amazement. White-gold stones against an azure blue sky, soaring columns and great vaulted domes, the power and the glory of ancient Rome.

To the left of the Temple of Jupiter is the much better preserved Temple of Bacchus, really one of the most complete we have seen, and here the detail and richness of imagination are fully visible. A most extraordinary ruin, if it can be called that—and, in fact, it is rather extraordinary that Baalbek itself has survived war and violence, both of which have ravaged its immediate environment.

Really, seeing Baalbek, I felt again what I experienced in Cairo after climbing the pyramids and seeing the phenomenal collection of objects, jewellery and mummies in Cairo's museum—what's left to build and craft after this? The skill and sophistication of both the most intricate gold-work and the sheer accomplishment of the pyramids, the temples and the sarcophagi, have we really improved on them at all? So, too, with Etruscan pottery and glass, jewellery and coins, Roman cities and temples, all made thousands of years ago with 'primitive' technology and tools. But the imagination was sublime, and the skills finely developed. And much the same can be said of all ancient civilizations.

I'm glad Baalbek was last on our list in Lebanon, because it would have been difficult to better it. And the next day we left by road for Damascus, the oldest continuously inhabited city in the world.

Hasna came over in the morning to see us off, and we spent a very pleasant hour or more chatting about all sorts of things—the truly amazing compendium of Arab women's writing that she, Radwa and Feryal Ghazoul have published, its translation into English, and now the work they are doing on volume two, which will contain excerpts and introductions to them. It reminded me of the two *Women Writing in India* volumes, and the *Women Writing in Africa* that Florence Howe and the Feminist Press pioneered nearly a quarter century ago. Whew, what a sobering thought!

And we talked about how difficult it is for independent young women today to find male companionship that respects their independence and treats them as equals. You wouldn't think we live in two quite different societies, the predicaments are so similar.

I was sorry to leave Beirut, but happy to have been able to see so much of the country and really happy to have re-established contact with Hasna after twelve years.

It's a two-hour journey by road from Beirut to Damascus, and we sort of retraced our steps from the day before, because the route is more or less the same as that to Baalbek. But the minute you enter Syria, the landscape changes. Arid, dusty, with low hills, and a *very* cold wind from the mountains. Damascus is much less affluent-looking than Beirut, buildings are modest, the city less chaotic, more orderly—and very clean. And such a gracious people; even the immigration officer who stamped our passports at the border, said 'Indian? Welcome.' And so it was, wherever we went: from India? Welcome. Such a warm and friendly comment.

Pogey's contact, via Ratish Nanda, at the Aga Khan Trust had booked us into one of those charming boutique hotels that are old Damascene houses in the predominantly Christian quarter of the Old City. We were in Dar al Yasmin in Bab Touma, a lovely old courtyard home, the courtyard now covered with a moveable canopy, all stone arches and tiled alcoves and niches, with the rooms arranged around three such courtyards. And of course, an orange tree in the centre, and a well. We saw many such houses, all belonging to affluent Damascenes of yore, and many now converted into hotels. The Old City is like old cities almost everywhere, with narrow streets and alleyways disappearing into open squares with churches, including Syrian Christian and Greek Orthodox, and our first evening there we heard chanting in Aramaic for the very first time. Wandered down several such alleys to reach Bab Sharqi, one of the gates to the Old City, and a wide street, clearly restored, with shops and cafés and hotels lining it.

It was clearly a busy tourist season because at least three restaurants we went to for dinner turned us away—they were booked solid. Finally, in a quiet side alley we found the Oriental Hotel, a beautiful old Damascene house, richly tiled and decorated, which had many, many tables in its very handsome courtyard, and we had an extremely nice dinner in very congenial surroundings. Walked back to Dar al Yasmin, streets still lively late at night, full of locals, some tourists, and men smoking hookahs and playing board games on the kerbside. Women, too, though more in cafés, less on the streets. Choc-a-bloc with carpet dealers, souvenir shops, pottery and silver, some very good.

More women than I had expected were in the hijab, both in Damascus and Aleppo, even younger women, covered from head to toe in drab black, brown, grey overgarments, heads completely covered, though wearing jeans and high heels below the hijab. I wonder if this is a class thing—do middle and upper class women also cover themselves? Hard to say, because we met none. Later, when I asked Baita from the Aga Khan Trust about this, she said, no, it cuts across class. But none of the young women at the Aga Khan Development Network (AKDN) were covered...Reports of the trendy upper crust are full of contradictions—elaborate veiled weddings with diamond accessories for the veils, making a fashion and status statement of a frankly discriminatory dress code for women. No Arab man is obliged to grow a beard in Syria, they wear western dress, smoke and drink, can't seem to live without music, and if their films are anything to go by, are as macho as they come. Not all women are covered, of course, but the streetscape is dotted with many who are, and shop windows are full of mannequins displaying varieties of the hijab.

Walked to the Grand Umayyid Mosque on the periphery of the Citadel, and near the Souk al Hamidiyeh. And what a very grand mosque it is. Nothing prepared me for the experience of walking into a mosque that is so clearly a Romanesque cathedral, not even Hagia Sophia in Istanbul, the best known of these churches-made-into-mosques. For one thing, the design is so evidently that of a cathedral, the chapel of St John the Baptist sits in the middle of the men's prayer hall, and all four sides of the building would have been covered with the most delicate mosaics. Only one wall and the main entrance now survive, but here the mosaics are gorgeous: cityscapes, such that we hadn't seen anywhere else, completely secular, in pale green and gold and beige, a touch of brown, the eye rested on them with real pleasure.

Friday noon prayers had just begun as we entered and continued for over an hour, with the most wonderful recitation of the Koran that I have ever heard. Deep and sonorous, and we sat in the huge courtyard and drank it in. Completely satisfying, like the ragis in a gurudwara. Truly, a sound to uplift the spirit. Outside the segregated prayer halls though, it was like a street, with children running and playing, families sitting around, people strolling—a kind of outing, it seemed, combined with a bit of religious observance.

Leaving the mosque, we wandered into the souk, but—it was closed! Friday. Still, having ventured in we walked around, and were struck by how spotlessly clean it is. Not a scrap of litter anywhere, amazing for this warren of streets and shops selling everything from spices and olives and herbs to mattresses and china and clothes and soap…Indeed, we noticed that, unlike our own Walled City, the Old City in Damascus is remarkably homogenous and relaxed. Although we were in the Christian quarter which has an astonishing number of churches, Damascus is predominantly Muslim, of course, like all of Syria; but as Adli Qudsi told us in Aleppo, all the sects and communities have learnt to live together—Kurds, Syrian Christians, Greek Orthodox, Shia and Sunni. Well, so it seems superficially, who knows what prejudices surface when tensions arise.

This was the first day we hadn't been on the road to somewhere or other, and it felt really nice, especially as we would be leaving for Aleppo the next day—by bus! Had dinner in a sweet little restaurant whose menu featured Crap Salad, Gordon Blue, Meat Blown Out, Lamp Shoops, Col Slow and Mushroom Chafing!! What on earth could the last one possibly be?

Buses in Syria are amazing. Cheap, efficient and frequent. Most of them are Chinese-made, probably private—there are dozens of companies plying the routes across the country and into Turkey, Lebanon and Jordan every day—and completely reliable. We paid SYP 250 (equal to Rs 250) each for a 300-km trip to Aleppo, and were served water and biscuits on the way! Like Turkey, where all buses have stewardesses!

Leaving Damascus, you realise just how arid and barren great swathes of the country are. Flat scrubland, with brown and sand-coloured hills stretching as far as the horizon, no agriculture, just olive trees in the slightly more hospitable regions, and—dust storms! Had quite forgotten what a duststorm feels like, but Damascus is very windy, and the dust swirls like it used to in Delhi years ago. Except around the Euphrates, where the land is fertile and irrigated; there's not much agriculture in the country, so what is the economy based on? Trading perhaps, some oil? A huge country with few resources but a small population (seventeen million) so I suppose there's enough.

That evening we walked from the hotel—in the new part of town but just at the edge of the Old City—to the mosque which I couldn't enter because I hadn't covered my head. Our hotel, the Ramsis, was located next to the auto parts market, for some reason, so we were obliged to walk past shop after shop of spare parts and tyres and sundry gadgets, till we emerged into streets with the most tantalising aromas—olive and laurel soap, coffee beans, dates and figs, dried apricots, mounds of green and black olives and mountains of goat cheese—a foretaste of the food and dry fruit we would find in the souks near the mosque. Afterwards we walked in the souk for a bit, till Adli Qudsi, a local contact of Pogey's in charge of the restoration of the Citadel and of Jdedieh, had us fetched to visit him in his office.

It's an artfully converted/restored old house, and later one of his employees, Anees, took us on a short but very interesting tour of this old part of Aleppo, something we would otherwise have missed. Adli told us that the work of the Aga Khan Trust for Culture (AKTC) and his office, together with the Syrian government, had focused on improving the infrastructure—sewage, water provision, 30 km of paved roads, electricity—and only after that, the restoration of buildings. This again, was the Christian quarter, clearly more upmarket than the old quarter around the mosque near the Citadel. But Aleppo is 90 per cent Muslim; and according to Adli, there is very little sectarian strife in Syria. He did, however, deplore the rise of religious fundamentalism. He was formal and a bit distant, but he arranged for us to go to Saint Simeon, a fifth-century church, the next day, and for his partner, Khaldoun Fasna, to take us on a tour of the Citadel.

Syria has the oldest recorded history in the world, going back as far as 2500–3000 BC at least—we saw the site of what was a Hittite Temple at the Citadel—much older than Harappa and the Indus Valley civilisation. One can only imagine the many layers that still need to be excavated, the richness of the history that will come to light. Ali Esmaeli at the AKTC in Aleppo said that of the estimated 10,000 archaeological sites in the country, only 3,000 had so far been excavated. Primarily by the French, followed by the Italians, and then Germans, Japanese, even Americans, in equal numbers. I must say, the French moved pretty quickly, seeing as how the French Mandate in the region only lasted for twenty years, from 1927 to 1947; they managed to entrench themselves pretty well. But their influence is much more visible in Lebanon than in Syria, because many street names are French, there are excellent patisseries and boulangeries all across the country, and of course, French schools both in Syria and Lebanon.

But the ruins are all ancient Roman, Ottoman, Ayubbid, Muslim in Syria—Lebanon, too—and even though the original European names have been Arabised (Antioch is now Antakia, Saint Simeon, Qalat Sa'man,

Heliopolis, Baalbek, Smyrna—in Turkey—now Izmir) the structures remain and vividly recall the complex overlapping, intertwined history of the Levant.

Saint Simeon is a fifth-century church perched atop a hill about 550 metres high, and is a memorial to Saint Simeon, an ascetic who gave rise to a following called the Stylites. The centrepiece of the monument is a pillar, hence, stylite (of which only a stump remains) on which Saint Simeon is believed to have lived and meditated, having renounced worldly and material comfort. His followers did likewise, but didn't, I think, live on pillars. All this sounded a bit over the top to me, but be that as it may, Saint Simeon's fame spread far and wide, and as time went on the original church was added to, expanded during the Crusades, and became a very grand monument indeed. Its plan is that of a rather squat cross, and only some of the walls, vaulted domes and apses are now extant, with the rest of the structure open to the sky.

There's something about a church or cathedral in ruin that returns it to nature in a most unexpected way. What originally impelled the worshipper to focus intently on the deity and his glory, to furnish and embellish the interior to the exclusion of all else and direct every utterance and song similarly, now must defer to a much more pagan spirit that inhabits this desolate space, visited sparsely and intermittently by those whose interest is merely transitory. A very different kind of reflection now takes place, a much more eclectic understanding of religion and history, man and God. The majesty of the church, imagined and recalled now in conjunction with an experience of other grand mosques and temples, situates it as fleeting and temporal, an apprehension that is only heightened by the fact that sky and wind and rain and storm now roam freely through it.

That afternoon we visited the Citadel of Aleppo with Khaldoun Fasna of the AKTC which, together with the Syrian Directorate General of Antiquities and Museums has restored it to some of its original magnificence. It is one of the most remarkable examples of military architecture in the Middle East, and certainly the most ancient. Built in the manner of a fortification and fortified city, it rises from the Old City, surrounded by a moat and approached by a steep ramp through an enormous gate. Though the discovery of the Hittite temple to the storm god dates it to the third millennium BC, the majority of the structures now visible are from the twelfth and thirteenth centuries, built by the Greeks, Romans, Byzantines, Ayubbids, Mamluks and Ottomans. We spent a fascinating hour or more wandering through the ruin with Khaldoun, marvelling at the fact that they had managed this enormous restoration in just under ten years, considering the monument had been buried under a mountain of earth and no one could guess what lay underneath.

The grandest of the structures is clearly the Great Mamluk Throne Hall, with Damascene mosaic inlaid, wood-panelled walls, stained glass, intricate marble tiling and vast proportions. But the most pleasing to me was the Big Mosque with its three Aleppine pine trees and quiet serenity. Could have stayed and contemplated there for hours.

Returned to the Ramsis Hotel via a walk through the souk and a completely authentic, dhaba-type Syrian lunch at one of the cafés across the Citadel.

In some respects, our last morning in Damascus was the most memorable. Baita, a young archaeologist from the AKTC, took us to see three Damascene homes that they are currently surveying and restoring. And they were lovely. We had seen several such in the Christian quarter, but these three, all in the Muslim section, were special. If you ask me how special, it would be difficult to explain because, apart from Beit Quwalty, there was nothing very different about them. But the proportions, the scale, the planting in the courtyards—orange and loquat trees, luxuriant, tumbling bougainvillea, heady, scented, wild rose creepers—and the exquisite tile work were just beautiful. The AKTC has its work cut out for itself, but I can't think of a more inspiring location for a site office! You just can't imagine, from the street outside, what a wonder awaits you as you enter the first courtyard.

Walking back through the souk Baita took us to one of the oldest caravanserais in the city, the Khan Asad Pasha serai, a majestic building in black and white stone, high-domed with a well in the centre of the courtyard, and elegant arched rooms arranged all along the upper storey. A more gracious halting place would be difficult to find, but Baita assured us these were not unusual! Both camels and people would have been happy to rest there…

To say this trip was special would be a real understatement, but I wonder what exactly made it different from our other travels in that region, from Turkey, Egypt, Morocco... Both Turkey and Egypt offer the same historical depth and layering of religion and culture, are rich in ruins and spectacular archaeological and architectural wonders, and present a vibrant modernity, as well. Morocco, too, even though its experience of colonisation and its proximity to Spain and the Arab conquests there, give it a somewhat different aspect.

One reason for what we felt must surely lie in the palpable social and political tension in both Lebanon and Syria, close to the surface and likely to sizzle at any moment. The day the UN Tribunal acquitted the five Syrian generals accused of plotting Rafik Hariri's assassination, for instance, Hasna warned us not to venture into the heart of Beirut because there could be violence. Wherever we walked or drove in the city there were checkpoints and diversions, and any number of spots marked X, the site of one violent death or another. Indeed, most recent 'memorable' events in Lebanon have been marked by terrible violence, either on the part of resisters or perpetrators. Everything seems to teeter on the brink of uncertainty and imminent disruption.

Although we didn't come across the same kind of volatility in Syria then, there is no mistaking that it is virtually a police state, people are repressed in subtle and not-so-subtle ways, and questions on the political situation are met with polite demurrence. Hasna said she hadn't been to Damascus in over two years because she was afraid she would be picked up on arrival—she was a signatory to a protest statement on the 155 Syrian intellectuals, writers and activists who had been jailed for expressing their dissident views on diverse issues.

And unlike the electoral and ethnic pluralism of Lebanon, Syria is very much the domain of the Assads, with large posters of Assad père et fils (father and son) plastered all over the country. Plus it's almost always in the eye of a political storm, being the target of US ire, as well as the ideological and strategic ally of Iran.

It was this apprehension of the fault-lines in both countries, evident even to a casual visitor and on superficial experience, that I think sets them apart. And in that, what remains as a strong impression is their equally evident dignity and grace.

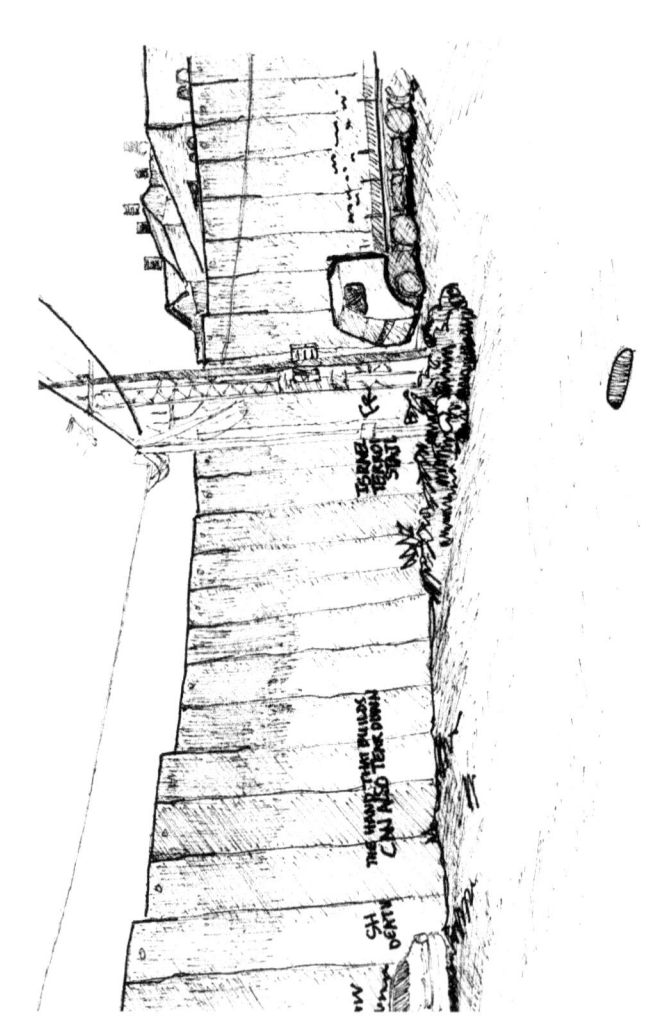

The Apartheid Wall in Jerusalem

Palestine: Grace Under Repression

May 2010

Jerusalem on the morning of Sunday, 2 May, on the veranda of the Legacy Hotel on Nablus Road, East Jerusalem. In the distance and above a clear blue sky, minarets and church spires, because the old city with its Christian, Arab and Muslim quarters is just a stone's throw away…

But historic, Biblical, ancient Roman and Arab Jerusalem is still only a dimly recalled lesson in my mind; I haven't experienced it yet. What grabbed me by the throat last night was the resilience and vibrancy and sheer staying power of the Palestinian writers who spoke, and their compatriots who came to listen. Snatches of experience and impressions, pain and its distillation recounted with humour, with anger, with sorrow or dignified restraint, lodged with razor-sharp clarity in my mind, surrounded by a sea of questions. And Najwan Darwish's poem, 'Reserved'.

> *Once I tried to sit*
> *On one of the vacant seats of hope*

> *But the word 'reserved'*
> *Was squatting there like a hyena*
>
> *(I did not sit down; no one sat down)*
> *The seats of hope are always reserved.*

This is PalFest 2010, the Palestine Festival of Literature, initiated by Ahdaf Soueif, the well-known Egyptian writer, and now in its third year. It's a festival with a difference, with a clear political purpose in addition to a literary focus, an attempt to expose international writers to the situation within Palestine, and to give Palestinians an opportunity to listen to them, exchange experiences and ideas and share their concerns. It's a festival that travels to Palestinians in different cities, recognising how difficult it is for them to move from one town to the next, given the restrictive system of permits, IDs and checkpoints that they have to negotiate. This year, PalFest's forty participants visited Nablus, Bethlehem, Hebron and Ramallah in addition to Jerusalem.

At the very same time, West Jerusalem is hosting *its* International Writers' Festival of Literature with participants like Amos Oz, David Grossman and Paul Auster, and later, Margaret Atwood and Amitav Ghosh, vying with PalFest's Henning Mankell, Geoff Dyer, Suheir Hammad, Suad Amiry, Victoria Brittain, Ahdaf Soueif, Raja Shehadeh, Selina Hastings, Nathalie Handal and many others. The question of any of them crossing over to be part of the other festival simply doesn't arise, given PalFest's solidarity with PACBI, the Palestine Campaign for the Academic and Cultural Boycott of Israel.

My eye falls on the visiting card given to me by Mordechai Vanunu the previous evening. It says:

FREEDOM AND ONLY FREEDOM I NEED NOW
Kidnapped from Rome September 30, 1986
After 18 years in Israeli prison
Waiting in East Jerusalem to be FREE
To leave—to see the world

Vanunu is the well-known Israeli physicist accused by the government of selling information about Israel's nuclear capability.

It's hard to conjure up the Biblical aura of the city, the Stations of the Cross, Via Dolorosa, the passion of Christ, as you enter the Old City through the Damascus Gate (the only gate now open, the other three being closed), down the sweeping arc of stone steps, polished smooth by centuries of pilgrims and inhabitants. Pavement vendors enticing you to their wares—boxes of ripe peaches, apricots, watermelons, dates and figs. An ancient woman with deep green grape leaves spread out in front of her. 'How much?' asks Suheir. 'Too much,' she replies dismissively… Suheir persists. 'They're cheaper in Bethlehem,' says the old woman, conceding the point, and making another one: food is expensive in Palestine. Almost everything comes from Israel.

Inside, the streets of the Old City are thick with people, with tourists, with devotees on Bible tours, many with Star of David badges on their T-shirts and caps. There are 45,000 inhabitants in the one sq km area of the Old City, divided into the Muslim, Christian, Armenian and Jewish quarters. An old British trick of dividing people on the basis of religion, dating back to the British Mandate in Jerusalem. Those old divisions, overlaid now by immigrant settlers, elbowing their way into Arab Jerusalem. It is a fiercely contested city.

In 1967, soon after the Israeli Occupation, 183 homes in the Old City were destroyed in order to create a public plaza. That plaza now houses 4,000 Jewish families, Star of David flags flying from their roofs, their homes barbed and fenced, with private security guards—twenty guards for each section of the settlement—and surveillance cameras filming everything. The settlements are at the edge of the Muslim quarter.

Right around the corner, or so it seems, one is pulled up short by possibly the oldest building in the Old City, the Ethiopian Monastery, its chapel bearing some of the adornments of eastern churches, seen in all their splendour in the Holy Sepulchre Church nearby. Here, now, in this modest space are large naïve paintings of the Queen of Sheba come to King Solomon, bearing gifts and offerings, the legends all in Amharic.

A Bible Tour group gathers in the large courtyard outside the Ethiopian Monastery, and just in front of the Holy Sepulchre drops to its knees and starts praying. They're from India. Kerala, it looks like. The place is studded with churches—the Greek and Latin Patriarchates, the Armenian and Ethiopian, the Maronites; the Church of Flagellation, of St Mary Magdalene, the Church of the

Redeemer, St Saviour Church, even Virgin Mary's Birth Church and the Church of All Nations. But it also has the Muslim Holy of Holies, the Al Aqsa Mosque at the Dome of the Rock, its golden globe visible from all points of the city. Visible, but closed to all Palestinians who are not Jerusalem residents, and even then, to all Jerusalemite men below the age of forty-five.

Suheir, fey, waif-like, with the Song of Songs in her heart, takes me on a tour of the Holy Sepulchre where she comes every morning when she's in Jerusalem. She's working on a long poem on the Queen of Sheba and her research has taken her far back in time, in myth, to uncover links with ancient Egypt that may well be considered heretical.

It's an Eastern Church, hung with low lanterns and chandeliers, aglow with Byzantine mosaics that gleam in the cool gloom of the interior. We pause in front of the spot on the floor where Christ's body was bathed by Mary Magdalene after it was taken down from the Crucifix. Another group of Bible tourists kneels down to kiss the stone. We move on, away from the crowds, to wander into sections made their own by the Greeks, the Armenians, the Christians, the Jews. The Church is divided up into quarters like the Old City, but less antagonistically, it seems. No checkpoints in the House of the Lord.

* * *

I doubt that I will ever again be able to utter that innocuous word 'Occupation' with equanimity. In Palestine it hits you smack between the eyes, trips you up, ties you down. You can never get enough distance between it and yourself. It's hard, when 90 per cent of your land is under the Israelis, and only 10 per cent can be claimed as your own—with their permission. When the colour of your Identity Card—blue for Jerusalem, green for the West Bank, brown for Gaza—determines your mobility *within your own country*, when there are 570 checkpoints controlled by the Israeli Defence Forces in the tiny area of the West Bank. Raja Shehadeh, the highly regarded Palestinian writer, author of *Palestinian Walks*, says:

> Where I live, not only has a mere 5900 sq km been divided into 227 geographical areas, I also live next to a people some of whom show signs of derangement with which they try to infect us. Some sixty years ago they cleared away an entire nation and thought that by renaming their ancient places they would wipe clean the slate of history. Those who tried to return were called infiltrators and shot. A new military order, No. 1650, just passed, defines all Palestinians living in the Israeli-occupied West Bank as infiltrators.

When I said cheerfully over the phone to Suad Amiry, my writer friend, 'See you soon in Jerusalem,' she replied gently, 'I'm not allowed into Jerusalem, Ritu, I'll see you in Nablus.'

On Victory Day, May 1945, David Ben-Gurion entered a quotation from the Prophet Hosea (9:1) in his diary: 'Do not rejoice, O Israel; do not be jubilant like the other nations.' And on the day after the surrender he wrote,

'Victory Day. Sad, very sad.' Ben-Gurion reckoned that Britain would no longer fulfil its commitments to Zionism, and that meant war with the Arabs. 'I began to prepare for war,' he wrote to his wife, Paula.

The war begun then, in 1948, the year of the Palestinian Naqba, has been waging ever since.

Were the Arabs mistaken in refusing UN Resolution 181 in 1948, which assigned 48 per cent of historic Palestine to the Palestinians and 49 per cent to the Zionists? Could they have forestalled the appropriation of 78 per cent of their land by the immigrants? Could they have foreseen the erosion of their farms, the nibbling away of their territory, the assault of the settlements?

All the What Ifs of history…

Land. Not any old land, the Holy Land. Who can claim it, who owns it, who controls it, who appropriates it, who is dispossessed…Suad says, 'I tell you, Ritu, the Israelis, they say, "Peace, peace, peace", but they take land, land, land.'

Land for roads, land for the settlers, land for the Wall, for the righteous, land that is rearranged…The Palestinian–American writer, Susan Abulhawa's book, *Mornings in Jenin,* from which she read in Jerusalem, opens with:

> In a distant time, before history marched over the hills and shattered present and future, before wind grabbed the land at one corner and shook it of its name and character…a small village east of Haifa lived quietly on figs and olives, open frontiers and sunshine.

The landscape is Biblical. Low hills, rich in the pale ivory stone that all Palestinian buildings are made of, but scrabbly and quite barren otherwise. Except for the olive trees which dot the hills and valleys, yielding the most luscious of olives, the lightest and clearest of oils.

Olives. Almonds. Pomegranate. Loquat. The grapes of Hebron and the apricots of Beit Jala…a cornucopia of fruit from a land under siege, a land divided by a wall.

The Wall—600 km of electrified concrete slabs, eight metres high, topped with razor wire, arc lights, surveillance cameras, encircling the West Bank, snaking through fields and olive groves, through city streets, alongside homes, dividing friends and families, erecting barriers and checkpoints. The Israelis call it a 'security fence', a protection against suicide bombers; the Palestinians call it the Apartheid Wall. Estimated to have cost USD 3.2 billion, it is two-thirds complete, and its human and economic costs have been staggering. Thousands of olive trees, some over 600 years old, have been uprooted; hundreds of thousands of villagers dispossessed, their farming at a standstill. The Wall is supposed to follow the contours of the Green Line—the ceasefire line of 1967—but it doesn't. Whenever an illegal or new settlement on Palestinian territory needs to be 'protected' by being drawn into 'Israel' the Wall goes around it, confiscating more Palestinian land in the process.

The irony of the Wall is that it was the brainchild of the Israeli left, vigorously opposed by the right because they feared it would eventually demarcate the Palestinian state from the Israeli one. In the event, it has succeeded in isolating and entrapping any number of villages, and squeezing the towns of Jerusalem, Bethlehem and Ramallah into smaller and smaller zones called 'envelopes'.

Our first sighting of the Wall was in Abu Dis in East Jerusalem, on the Al Quds University campus. Right by the football field which it would have bisected, annexing almost one-third of the campus, if it hadn't been for strenuous resistance by the students. The shock of seeing it looming ahead as you make your way to the Museum of Mathematics pulls you up short. Covered with graffiti— 'This is a wall of shame. But what goes around must come around'; 'Solidarity is the only answer,' and 'Palestine will be free!'—and as far as the eye can see, row upon row of the Keys of Return, symbol of the refugees' right to return to their homes. Idyllic pastoral scenes have been painted next to masked militants reflecting both the hope and the hopelessness of their predicament.

Hard by is the Museum of Political Prisoners, one of the few I've ever seen. Despite the harrowing nature of its subject and the gruesome accounts of torture and detention, it's a strangely uplifting space. The walls are covered with posters of defiance and resistance, many of surprising sophistication in draughtsmanship and conceptualisation. Declarations like, 'I will kiss the ground of my cell because it is part of my homeland' throw a challenge both to the fact of imprisonment and to the Israeli state that has occupied—usurped—the homeland. That is hellbent on changing the facts on the ground.

And there is disquiet in the air. At Al Quds, at the edge of Jerusalem, which the Zionists insist will be an undisputed part of Israel, the student body votes 43 per cent Hamas, and roughly 50 per cent of the women wear the hijab.

It is illegal for Israelis to enter the West Bank, for Palestinians to go to Israel; both are punishable offences. Road signs everywhere prohibit entry and exit, Israeli roads are barred to Palestinians, Palestinians cannot repair or tar their roads without Israel's permission. On the road to Nablus, north of Jerusalem, the contrast couldn't be sharper. Broad, smooth, beautifully maintained roads on the Israeli side stretching towards the settlements, mostly empty because only cars with Israeli licence plates are allowed to use them. At traffic intersections, the speeding cars of settlers have right of way, even though the roads have been built on Palestinian land and paid for with Palestinian taxes. In any case, Palestinian vehicles aren't likely to overtake them—their roads are pitted and potholed, caved in at places, with street vendors and pavement shops lining the edges. Somehow, the feeling of abandonment is inescapable.

* * *

Between 2002 and 2008, Nablus was closed and curfewed. The Israeli Defence Force (IDF) conducted raids every day and economic activity was frozen. Before the economic blockade of Nablus by Israel 100,000 people commuted to the city; it was the commercial hub of the West Bank. It was also the centre of militancy, the locus of the First and Second Intifadas. Walking through the old city, the walls are plastered with posters of the martyrs, all posed before they took off on their missions. It's striking how many young and unshaven faces peer out at you from them and indeed, a good part of a generation has been lost to the cause of liberation.

The refugee camp at Balata was set up in 1950 after the 1948 Naqba on a one-sq-km piece of land leased to United Nations Refugee Welfare Association (UNRWA) by the villagers of Balata for ninety-nine years. Six thousand refugees camped in tents which were replaced by rooms after twenty years, but regular water supply and sewage arrived much later. Today, there are 25,000 people living in the camp area, which now has its own schools, hospital, cultural centre and cemetery. Walking through the entire camp area, I was struck by the fact that it looks like any other densely populated inner city habitation—Chandni Chowk is more crowded, dirty and unkempt. But, yes, the dwellings are piled up on top of each other, alleys little more than three feet wide separate buildings, and decay and neglect are evident. At the time of the Second Intifada in 2000, the IDF killed 230 people in Balata, and there are still 480 in Israeli prisons, several convicted for life. Every one of the 800 families in the camp lost a son, brother, father or uncle to the Intifada, and Israel's economic blockade of Nablus resulted in 40 per cent unemployment in the camp.

In the 1970s, Israel had opened the borders and allowed Palestinian labour into Israel, which helped raise the income of the refugees. After the First Intifada, however, the percentage of Palestinians working in Israel fell from 60 per cent to 30 per cent; and the camp at Balata, till as recently as 2009, was enclosed by barbed wire fencing. All entrances, bar one, were closed. When the fencing was removed and repair work began on the roads, the Israelis insisted that they be made 'tank-width', in the event of a third uprising.

That evening at the Turkish Hammam in Nablus, Suad regaled us with an account of her eighteen-hour midnight journey across the border into Israel with twenty-four labourers, all entering Israeli territory illegally, in order to work. She disguised herself as a man, borrowed her husband's clothes, stuffed her hair under a baseball cap, and set off on the trek. 'After every kilometre or two,' she said, 'Murad would tell me to duck in order to avoid the soldiers at the barriers who would shoot at sight. Shoot? I thought, my God, Suad, what have you started?' There was no going back, however, so she stuck it out, and at dawn they crossed over. But of the original party of twenty-four only four made it—the rest had been arrested. And the adventure provided Suad with the material for her newest book, *Nothing to Lose But Your Life*.

Yet, my strongest sensory impression of Nablus is of the oldest spice shop in the old city, a cool, dark, vaulted building, room after room filled with bags and sacks of fresh zatar, saffron from Turkey and Iran, turmeric, sage, marjoram, thyme and rosemary; huge troughs where wild thyme was being roasted before being ground with sesame seeds to make the aromatic and indispensable garnish of zatar; dried mushrooms and exotic herbs, whole red chillies and oregano…an absolute heaven of aroma and colour.

At An Najah University next morning, I was completely taken aback by the sight of an auditorium filled to capacity with fully veiled female students. As in other universities we visited—in Jerusalem, Bethlehem, Ramallah and Hebron—women make up 50 per cent or more of the student body, but the Nablus campuses are the most conservative, at least as far as dress codes are concerned. And it was only in An Najah that Suheir and I came face-to-face with male students (and even, tacitly, some faculty) who justified honour killings. 'If I find my sister has done something wrong,' said one of them in our workshop, 'I will kill her.'

Despite my asking the many Palestinian writers we met about the increasing use of the hijab by young women, I never did get a satisfactory explanation.

But everywhere we went, the venues were packed to capacity. At the stunning palace of Qasr Qasem atop a hill in Nablus, superbly restored by Suad Amiry (she's an architect and conservator in real life), there were people hanging over the parapets, perched in alcoves and crowded into niches, to hear what the writers and poets had to say.

* * *

There is no escaping the confluence—and now the conflict—of religions in the Holy Land, and Bethlehem, with the Church of the Nativity, situated opposite the Mosque of Omar in the largest and most gracious square in the city, is redolent with all. Greek. Armenian. Syrian. Coptic. Ethiopian. Impossible not to be affected by the sublime grace and glory of the Nativity in the Church, with its magnificent soaring interior, hung with glittering chandeliers, arras, glowing lanterns and jewel-like mosaics. The crypt where Christ was born is marked only by a silver star on the ground, but the one where the Three Magi offered myrrh, frankincense and gold, not even that. Yet the charge is unmistakable.

As is the great uplifting of the spirit on hearing the *azaan* soaring up from the minaret of the mosque when we emerge from the church into the square. Can there be anything more musical and noble than a single voice raised to the heavens, calling the devout to prayer? Only the choir, it seems to me.

Bethlehem, so sacred to Christians and Jews and of such ancient piety, is almost completely encircled by the Wall, choking it off from the surrounding areas, scarring the landscape, cutting right through the town in arbitrary twists and turns. Homes find themselves enclosed, their inhabitants having to make a detour of up to 10–12 km to reach places that are literally, a few yards away.

The Reverend Mitri el-Raheb took us on a Wall tour, surely one of the most disturbing tours I have ever been on. The Wall is everywhere. Wherever you turn, it looms up against you. Beside you, behind you, in front of you, in the distance too, because you can see it snaking its way across farmland and hills. Gracious dwellings are foreshortened by the Wall, staring its graffiti in the face.

'I didn't ask to be born Palestinian, I just got lucky,' says one. 'Palestine will win,' says another. And a few feet away is a portrait of the young Yasser Arafat, Abu Amar, in his thirties, his distinctive kaffiyeh around his head, rifle in hand.

The Wall is constructed just at the edge of where the last houses on city streets end, thus ensuring that the city cannot grow. Ensuring also that farming families cannot easily access their land—and if land lies uncultivated for seven years, it is confiscated. But how can one cultivate it when access is strictly regulated and the water wells are beyond reach? Israeli law says, moreover, that if stones and rocks comprise more than 50 per cent of the land it is unfit for agriculture (but the olive trees don't mind); that the Israeli government has the right to confiscate land if it is required for new roads (which means roads for the new settler communities); that the Israeli government has the right to confiscate land to install pipelines or sewage systems for the new communities (the illegal settlers).

Shareef Khalid, a 67-year-old farmer and representative of the Land Defence Committee in Qalqilia district on the western border with Israel, reports the following exchange between his neighbour and the Israeli commander who was bulldozing his neighbour's land:

> 'Why are you uprooting my trees?' the farmer asked.
> 'These trees are owned by the government, they are not yours,' replied the commander.
> 'How did they come to be owned by the government? I am the rightful owner.'

'That is not my business,' said the commander.
'Can I sell your car?' asked the farmer.
'Of course not!' replied the commander.
'Then who has the authority to sell my land?'
'That is not my business either.'

Qalqilia is almost completely enclosed by the Wall, an island in a sea of hostility.

The Reverend Mitri recounted several similar stories, from which it appears that the business of the Israeli government is to confine the Palestinians into smaller and smaller enclaves, encourage illegal settlements and demographically and otherwise, alter the facts on the ground. But in Benin in the north, resistance by the village and solidarity groups to the Canadian construction company, Green Park Corporation, has temporarily halted construction on the Wall in that area. A suit filed in the High Court in Montreal comes up for hearing on 3 June 2010.

* * *

South of Bethlehem, in Hebron, 1,500 IDF soldiers guard 400 settler families perched on hills around the city. In 1994, Baruch Goldstein, a settler from Brooklyn, stormed the Ibrahimi Mosque in Hebron during the dawn prayers and machine-gunned twenty-nine worshippers in the central hall. A curfew was imposed on the city for thirty days during which people were not allowed to leave their homes, and the mosque was closed for ten months. When it was reopened, it had been bisected into two: one area for

Muslims, the other for Jews, for the mosque compound is sacred to both: the tombs of Abraham, Isaac and Jacob lie within its precincts. And indeed the Hebron Jews are among the city's oldest inhabitants. Since the massacre, the IDF has barricaded the mosque and its environs, closed all eight entrances to it, bar one, which is elaborately 'secured', ostensibly to provide 'protection' to Palestinians praying in the mosque. In effect, however, it's like entering a high security facility or detention centre, not a place of worship.

The old city of Hebron, known in Arabic as al-Khalil (the friend), goes back to the Mamluk and Ayyubid eras, and presents all the architectural features of those dynasties—horseshoe arched windows, slender columns, beautifully decorated entrance doors to the buildings and impressive ironwork. Post the massacre, Hebron is now divided into two: H1, which is under the Palestinian Authority; H2 under the Israelis, where 4,500 Palestinians live. (As we walk through the deserted streets of H2, Suheir tells me, 'I call it H2 without O.'). The remainder of its population of approximately 200,000 (it's the largest city in the West Bank) lives in H1.

There are more soldiers of the IDF in Hebron than there are in Southern Lebanon; and it has 101 checkpoints in the one-sq-km area of the old city, where we are headed for the Ibrahimi Mosque. We walk through a typical souk lined with shops selling bric-a-brac, vegetables and fruit, groceries and provisions, and remark again on the graceful and elegant proportions of the market. Its harmony is rudely disrupted as we emerge into a street blocked off at one end by a turnstile, manned by soldiers. Only four people may enter at a time, even though it is time for the afternoon prayer and there are crowds of people waiting to go in. Woe betide if you forget your ID at home or have the wrong colour. Every single article you are carrying (including wallets, passports, even spectacles) has to be deposited and checked while you pass through metal detectors before you can enter the mosque. But when you do, you realise with a shock that this is a mosque without a courtyard—the courtyard has been blocked off by a steel partition, separating it from the main building. No Palestinian can enter it, it is Israeli military controlled.

I leave quickly. The tension in the mosque is unbearable.

Outside, H2 is a ghost town. The streets are silent, the shops have been ordered closed and are shuttered and barred. Many have Star of David graffiti on the doors. No Palestinian can walk on the roads that serve the settler communities encircling Hebron, and no Palestinian car is allowed to drive through. Soldiers with machine guns are perched on the deserted rooftops, and 360-degree surveillance cameras photograph every movement, twenty-four hours a day. Some roads are reserved for settlers; others, Palestinians are allowed to traverse on foot only; and a third kind, which they are allowed to drive through but cannot leave their vehicles on. From where we stand, we can see at least a couple of settlements in the near distance, flags fluttering, barbed wire fencing around them. Hebron is home to 400 settler families from the US (mostly from Brooklyn, NY) and Canada, whose migration to Israel and the West Bank was made possible through funds raised in the US especially for their resettlement, and who are completely subsidised by the state of Israel. They are the Hasidic and Haredim sects, their occupation—in every sense of the word—is Occupation, reclaiming the Holy Land, and their schooling is in yeshivas where studying the Talmud and Torah is their sole activity. Their orthodoxy rivals the fundamentalism of the Wahabis, and is every bit as repellant. What's more, it's funded by the Israeli government.

And Hebron is 'the real game'. A senior Israeli army officer is reported to have told the International Crisis Group that he 'would rather give back Tel Aviv than Hebron' which he described as 'Jewish land…promised to us by the Bible, by God.'

Not all settlers are in settlements, however. Walking back from the mosque we passed under the infamous wire netting that stretches across narrow streets, on which settlers who have constructed their homes above shops owned by Palestinians, throw their garbage, empty buckets of dirty water, urinate, and otherwise harass and humiliate those below them. Truly, there is something despicable about their inhumanity.

The Hebron Rehabilitation Committee was set up in 1996 under a Presidential decree passed by Yasser Arafat, with the express purpose of rehabilitating and repopulating the Old City. Over the years, and especially after the active Judaisation policies of the 1980s and the construction of new settlements around Hebron, Palestinians began leaving

Old Hebron in large numbers. In 1996 there were only 400 Palestinians left in the Old City; in the thirteen years that the Hebron Rehabilitation Committee has been working in H2, the population has increased to 4,500, and more than 800 homes have been restored. We walked on 5 km of new roads that have been laid, and through alleys that are now paved and lit. Heart-warming and encouraging signs, no doubt, and the HRC is nothing if not dedicated and resolute—but the settlements are growing apace, confirming that Hebron may indeed be the 'real game'.

* * *

This year, 2010, the IDF recruited 400 yeshiva graduates for various technical tracks in a project designed specifically for the Haredim. Another 500 men are part of a Haredi battalion. Major General Avi Zamir, head of the IDF's Personnel Directorate, says, 'Ten years ago if you had talked to the rabbis and political leaders of the Haredim about army service, they would have shown you the door…Today, the socio-economic situation of the Haredim is dire.'

The IDF may have succeeded in recruiting these Haredim into the armed forces (a felt need, as immigrants from Russia, the traditional recruits, were down to a trickle) but they have come up against all sorts of challenges to their authority from them, including refusing orders that require them to dismantle Jewish settlements. In October 2009, two recruits to the Shimson Battalion unfurled a banner at their swearing-in ceremony which declared: 'Shimson Does Not Evacuate Homesh.' Homesh is a settlement situated on a steep hill a few miles north-west of Nablus, and is one of the four West Bank settlements from which Israel withdrew in 2005, as part of Ariel Sharon's Gaza disengagement plan. Although the IDF keeps dispatching soldiers to remove them the settlers keep returning, opening a yeshiva, organising pilgrimages, and turning the ruins of Homesh into a symbol of their spiritual resolve.

The Shimson Battalion's refusal was followed by the Nahshon Battalion, and the Kfir Brigade which said: 'Kfir Does Not Expel Jews.' SOS Israel, an organisation of the far right, consistently and strenuously opposes ceding any part of the Holy Land to non-Jews; it held a ceremony in Jerusalem to award cash prizes of 20,000 shekels (roughly USD 5500) to the members of Shimson Battalion.

But it's not just the Zionist Haredim who are refusing to dismantle illegal settlements. The non-profit Israel Land Fund which seeks to increase Jewish presence in East Jerusalem, intends to encircle the Old City with a ring of Jewish settlements. Its efforts are focused on: walking into Palestinian buildings (that have been unoccupied because their owners live abroad) and moving Jewish families into them; and initiating plans to construct Jewish neighbourhoods in the heart of the Palestinian population.

Ha'aretz reports:'On the drawing board are hundreds of plans for housing units in various stages of approval, behind many of which stands the American Jewish gambling Moghul, Irving Moskowitz.' Jewish families already surround the Mount of Olives cemetery, and the Shimon Hatzadik neighbourhood is rapidly going up in Sheikh Jarrah. Aryeh King of the Israel Land Fund says:

The idea is to build layer after layer surrounding the centre, like an onion. Because like an onion, the longer it is in the fire, the sweeter it becomes—that's how Jerusalem is. The more pressure there is, the more good will come of it.

On our last day in Jerusalem we walk to Sheikh Jarrah, a short distance from the hotel, and find a family of women who have been parked on the pavement ever since they were evicted from their home in 2008. They are among the twenty-eight families of Sheikh Jarrah who have been dispossessed by Jewish settlers, who have been trying to gain possession of property that they claim was owned by Jewish families who have since left.

The women live on the pavement by day and used to sleep in makeshift tents at night till the tents were dismantled by the Israelis. They now sleep over with friends or neighbours, but return every morning to take up their vigil again. They belong to one of the four main families—the Al Kurd, Hanoun, Al-Ghawi and Rfhqa Al-Kurd—who have been forcibly evicted, and whose cases are being heard in court.

A few years ago, 150 Jewish families who live overseas and whose property in Jerusalem was being claimed by settlers and immigrants, signed a petition saying that their homes could be claimed only if and when Palestinian homes and property in Haifa and Jaffa were returned to their original owners. 'Just because those who want to claim our property are Jewish doesn't entitle them to take it over.'

All land in Sheikh Jarrah is under the jurisdiction of

the Israeli General Custodian. Sheikh Jarrah lies between the Old City and Mount Scopus, home to the Hebrew University, strategically located in the historic basin that people like Aryeh King believe is theirs by right.

Avraham Yehoshua, a writer who lives in Haifa, has lost three friends in attacks on the Hebrew University of Jerusalem and on Maxime's restaurant in Haifa. Although he supports the construction of the Wall, he disagrees strongly with Aryeh King:

> We left them 22 per cent of Palestine and now we've taken what's left. By increasing the settlements what we're saying to them is: 'You will be forever without citizenship in your own country.'…We have wounded them grievously and we should be fully aware of this.

Perhaps it's fitting that the last word be left to Raja Shehadeh, who said at the Turkish Hammam in Nablus:

> Israel is attempting to define the terrain, to claim and fragment it with wire fences, signposts, gates and roadblocks, staffed by soldiers backed up by tanks. I am but one of the millions of travellers who have passed through over the ages. I lifted my eyes and beheld the wonderful valley created aeons ago as it stretches far and long, north to Lebanon and south to the Red Sea and into Africa, utterly oblivious to the man-made borders that come and go.

Grace under pressure, I thought. Or should it be, under repression?

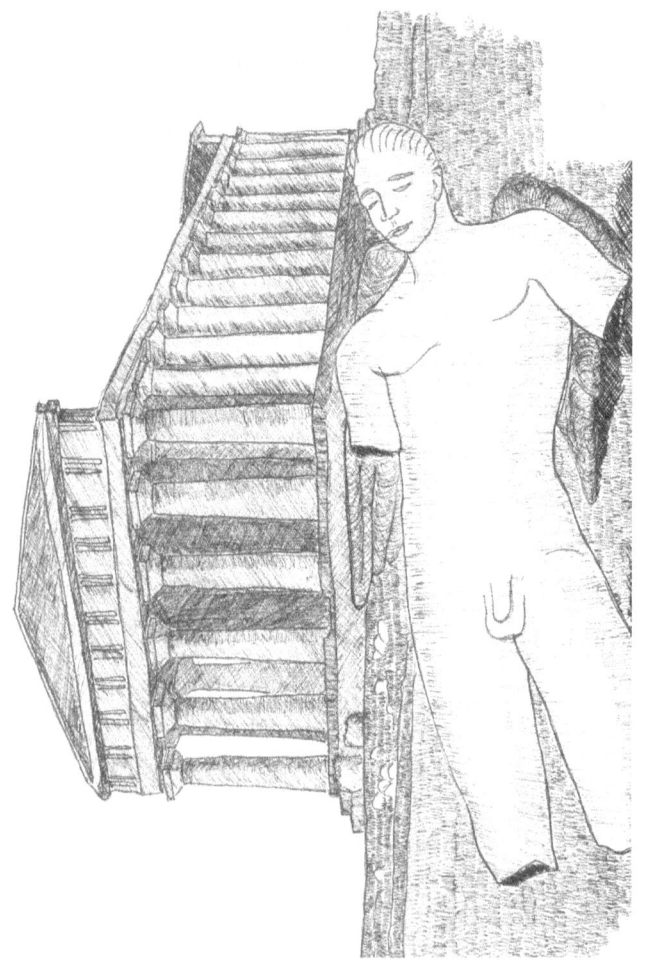

The Fallen Icarus in Agrigento

Sicily: Lampedusa Land

September 2012

I didn't think I would begin my trip to Sicily with a trip to the hospital, but that's what happened. Took a tumble on the stairs coming down from the bedroom of our little apartment, landed with a thud on my bottom, my foot twisted painfully under me.

That's all I needed to inaugurate the morning at Villa d'Acante in Nacalino, on the southern tip of Sicily. We would spend a week here, then drive across the island, stopping on the way at Agrigento and the Greek ruins, then make our way leisurely through Segesta, Selinunte and other musically named towns, to Palermo.

But the first stop turned out to be the general hospital at Modica. Having hobbled my way down the Corso in Modica, I decided to wait out the Ibla part of the day's tour at a little bar and watch the locals go by. No point aggravating the ankle or the fracture, if that's what it was, or the tendon or ligament or whatever…

It was a Sunday, so there was only one senior doctor on duty in Accident & Emergency, and about ten people ahead of me when Pogey and I arrived at around 5.30 p.m.

A very helpful young intern registered me, and asked us to wait while he tried to see if he could organise an X-ray of my foot without the senior doctor's authorisation. So we waited. And waited. And waited. Six o'clock, 6.30, 7 o'clock, 7.30. No doctor, no X-ray. People were being called in, but why weren't they coming out? And then after 7.30, no one was being called in either. The man ahead of me in the queue said he'd been there since 4.30! Oh dear. Should we just leave, sleep on it, and see what the foot looked like in the morning? But what if it was a fracture and needed a cast? Dreadful thought.

Antonella, who had accompanied us to the hospital, decided to collar the intern who had registered me, but he was dashing in and out of A&E, looking harried. And well he might. They were dealing with a major road accident—two cars, one on top of the other, and a third that collided with them. One patient serious, and the senior doctor was monitoring him. Ah. No telling how long this might take then.

Medical services are free across Italy, whether or not you have insurance. Yet few among those in real need—immigrants, mainly—ever go to a hospital, because once they're registered they're on the government scanner and are likely to be deported if they're illegal. A great number of Sicilian businesses and agricultural produce entrepreneurs employ such labour, primarily from Libya, Algeria, Tunisia…But mainly Libya. The general hospital at Modica is one of the few in the country that protects the status of anyone who comes to it because it desists from reporting them.

By now my ankle was throbbing painfully and all I wanted to do was have a stiff drink, put my feet up, and listen to the silence at Villa d'Acante. More and more worried faces were going in and out of the A&E swing doors through which I could see a clutch of patients and their family members waiting—well, patiently. Then suddenly the young intern appeared, waving a piece of paper at me and said, 'Go straight for your X-ray, doctor will see after.' But the only lift we could take to the X-ray room was almost half a kilometre of corridors away and I could barely manage a few steps. What to do? Grin and bear it. We set off, and by the grace of God (what else, in Italy?) a staff member appeared, unlocked a lift just a few feet away, muttering, 'What are they thinking of, sending you to that lift so far away'? and we got in thankfully.

This being Sunday the technicians in the X-ray department were normally off duty, but the emergency accident had one of them come in, the kindest old man, who did the job in a jiffy, asked me to wait while he developed the film, came out shortly and announced happily, 'Zero!' No fracture, no tissue damage, no torn tendons or ligaments, just what he called a 'minor distortion'! Phew. I could have hugged that technician. What a relief. And what luck. And it hadn't cost me a penny.

As we emerged from A&E and walked towards the car, another ambulance rolled in and a woman on a stretcher was wheeled out—it looked like a long night for the medicos at the hospital. Budget cuts for essential services have been so dramatic in Italy that most hospitals are seriously understaffed, with personnel having to do double duty. Sometimes even treble duty. All a result of the crisis in Europe.

We were eight at Nacalino. Simone and Erik from Paris, via Cipières; Roberto and Antonella from Rome; Rosalba from Como; Bunny from London; and Pogey and me. Filippo and Tina's apartments-on-rent on their estate, Villa d'Acante, are located in the kind of Sicilian countryside that is the setting for all those wonderful Andrea Camilleri novels, with his police officer Montalbano, working out of towns like the ones we were going to see—Scicli and Noto and Modica and Ragusa and…and also the kind of rural landscape that you imagine for all of Sicily. Dry, with drystone boundary walls, scrubby, but with acres and acres of olive trees, their silver-tipped leaves glinting in the sunlight. And in fact, the amount and varieties of olive oil (and olives) you get here would be hard to match. But it's the sky and the silence, both vast and unbroken that are the most amazing. Expansive and all-encompassing, stilling the agitations of the mind.

Post-fall, I limped my way through the charming town of Modica, west of Nacalino, with its magnificent Chiesa S. Giorgio (reached by climbing 250 steps, which of course, I couldn't attempt) on the hilltop, Modica Alta, and the less magnificent but imposing Chiesa S. Pietro at street level. All the towns reflect the topography of the country—hilly and flat, valleys between low hills, with the old town generally on the hill and the modern urban centro on flatter terrain. Modica is a World Heritage Site and one can understand why. Lovely baroque villas, mansions and palazzos, little streets opening out into beautifully spacious squares, now teeming with tourists. Like us. So visible in fact, that we wondered where the locals were! But they're around, obviously, because even in these tiny towns with tiny populations, it's hard to find a parking spot. And it's obviously a prosperous place.

* * *

Cannoli. A Sicilian delight, dolce, of course, made of a deliciously crisp envelope into which is filled the lightest, fluffiest, freshest ricotta which has been whipped into a heavenly and lightly sugared confection, topped with pistachios. Antonella, a connoisseur of cannoli, informed us that the best-ever cannoli was to be had only in Modica, and only at Antica Dolceria Bonajuto on Corso Umberto—or rather, off the Corso in one of those narrow creeper-hung streets. An old-world confectionery with wooden, glass-fronted cupboards, specialising in handmade chocolates made the Aztec way, and in cannoli. And, in season, candied orange-peel. Well, the cannoli was divine, as promised, and the chocolates were quite unique. Everywhere else in industrialised Europe, chocolates are produced mechanically; in Modica, the cocoa beans are ground between two stones, and instead of the traditional maize, sugar is added to give the chocolate an unexpected grainy consistency. Equally unexpected are the flavours— chilli pepper, salt, cinnamon, in addition to vanilla and orange essence.

We returned home to a yummy omelette cooked by Erik, together with the previous day's leftovers—anchovies, olives, pickled tomatoes, ham and cheese, and a tuna-potato-capers salad that Antonella conjured up in three minutes flat. Peaches and grapes and Aztee chocolates to wrap it all up.

My foot having benefited enormously from a night's sleep, we set off the next day for Noto (another World Heritage Site), about one hour east and north of Nacalino, with a long street of baroque mansions, red-gold buildings which gleam and glow in the evening light, as they do in all the towns, especially when the setting sun strikes the façades of the churches. And all the towns date back mostly to the eighteenth century, rebuilt after the great earthquake of 1693 when almost everything in Sicily was razed to the ground.

Noto used to be a tuna town, its baronial mansions the homes of the tuna kings who made their money from the tuna fishing that was the mainstay of the district. The seas have been fished to near-depletion now and Noto, like many other Sicilian towns, is supported substantially by tourism. Churches and mansions—we were struck by just how many churches these small towns boasted, often as many as seven or eight for populations of under one million, or even less than 50,000—many abandoned or permanently closed now, like the very many boarded-up homes we saw across the country. Migration out of the country is fairly high, because employment is hard to find if you have skills that are marketable. And yet immigrants flock to the cities here, willing to do the menial labour that the locals won't.

This being tuna town, we decided to go down to Marzememi by the coast, where all the tuna factories were located, now mostly in disuse. But the term 'factory outlet' here acquires a completely different meaning—warehouse spaces crammed with the most delectable fish produce. Dried. Pickled. Smoked. Sliced and steeped in oils and herbs. Fish eggs of unimaginable variety. Tomatoes in every shape and size and flavour, sundried, halved and quartered, shredded and seasoned, the aromas filling the space and suffusing the senses. And pesto—with pistachio and pine nuts and olives and rosemary. The olives themselves, like jade and black marbles in their jars. Mushrooms and cheeses and tins and tins of anchovies, we could have spent the whole afternoon in this piscatorial heaven.

But Scicli beckoned, so we set off for this baroque town, just 10 km south-west of Modica, where some of the Montalbano episodes were shot, notably in the building that now houses the offices of the Municipio. And, indeed, we saw the room in which Inspector Montalbano's 'office' was located, a sad sort of baroque memory, yet oddly evocative. Churches and mansions again, and again a whiff of old splendour.

I'm not one for baroque, even at its best. And if ever proof was needed that the style really is a bit over the top, the churches in Scicli provide it in abundance. The Chiesa di San Matteo, for instance, is so overloaded with every kind of embellishment and adornment that it could have qualified for what John (Bissell, of Fabindia fame) once called 'early Karol Bagh'. Genuine kitsch, not the camp variety that now passes for 'art'.

But the Chiesa S. Giovanni in Modica Alta is sublime—a steep climb to the top of the hill where it stands supreme, flanked at every landing by bougainvillea, jasmine and wisteria spilling over, resplendent with colour. Its interior is eggshell blue and white and gold, graceful stucco on its walls, dome and vaulted ceiling, the epitome of majesty and grace. An unmistakably baroque façade, but inside, restrained and elegant.

Like the exquisite Chiesa Matrice in Erice, near Segesta. A tiny hill town perched on an isolated limestone spur, 751 metres above the Mediterranean. Often shrouded in a mist known as Venus' veil, the guidebook said. Matrice has a beautiful fifteenth-century Gothic exterior (those stone churches are simply wonderful) and the most breathtaking cream stucco work on the vaulted ceiling. Like ivory lace. A wedding dress. How could they have bypassed baroque excess in 1852, when this elaborate carving was done, and created something so supremely and unexpectedly *right*? But the most appealing in my view, both aesthetically and otherwise, are those churches built on top of Greek temples or mosques, without demolishing what had been there earlier. The main Duomo in Siracusa, for instance, is remarkable for the Doric columns you see on the sides of the church, some complete, some in halves, none concealed. Or the distinctly Moorish façade of the great Norman cathedrals in Palermo and Monreale, and the unmistakeably Islamic geometric motifs in the mosaics on the floor and on the walls—even a mihrab in delicate outline on one wall in the Monreale church. Unselfconscious and matter of fact. No fuss, no breast-beating or chest-thumping, just a simple acknowledgement of a different history, a different religion.

Can one even imagine such a possibility in temple, church or mosque today?

You think of Sicily as sparse—and poor. But the towns are densely packed, every available space built-up. The soil is rich and dark, volcanic, so very fertile, and the countryside now has miles and miles of plastic greenhouses under which grow tomatoes and grapes and fruit and vegetables for export. It's true that there are large stretches in central Sicily that are dry and brown, where only the hardy olive trees survive (and thrive, it must be said) but even so, there must have been great wealth to support all those churches and noble estates. An extreme and resolute feudalism must have appropriated the greater part of this bounty, for there were no less than 750 feudal families on this small island, as we found when we saw all their emblems displayed in the Castello at Donnafugata, where Giuseppe di Lampedusa's *The Leopard* was filmed.

Enter the Mafia. As early as the fifteenth century, restrictive commercial opportunities were so stringent in Sicily that even the over-privileged feudals were forced to make changes in order to survive. They introduced a policy of resettlement that forced thousands of peasants off the land and into new towns. The feudals themselves moved to large cities, leaving the job of collecting rents to their bailiffs. The bailiffs in turn employed the early Mafiosi—small gangs of armed peasants—to do the dirty work. And although they were feared by the peasantry, they were also supported by them because they were destablising the feudal system by robbing the large estates as well. This 'common cause' became the origin of the term Cosa Nostra (Our Thing), and the code of protection or silence (Omerta), the peasants' way of protecting the Mafiosi from the police.

In time, the Mafia entered everything—banking, construction, narcotics, food, you name it. Then in the 1980s the anti-Mafia movement gained strength and the Mafia kingpin, Salvatore (Toto) Riina, was arrested and sentenced to life imprisonment. In 1986, following four years of interrogation of another Mafia boss, Tommaso Buscetta, by the Palermo magistrate, Giovanni Falcone, 500 top Mafiosi were put on trial in a specially constructed bunker near Palermo's Ucciardone prison; 347 were convicted, nineteen were sentenced to life imprisonment, and their combined jail terms totalled 2,665 years.

Needless to say, the Mafia retaliated by killing top investigators like Paulo Borselino, Carlo Alberto Dalla Chiesa and a Modica priest, Giuseppe Puglisi, all of whom they saw as threats. Still, the tightening of the screws by the authorities has had some success, and many of the agricultural co-operatives that run the agriturismo project of the Sicilian government have been developed on land seized by it from the Mafiosi. So, though still active, Mafia presence today is more 'integrated', a little less inclined to banditry. All this fascinating information courtesy my *Lonely Planet*. (In Noto, Antonella bought me a copy of Roberto Saviano's book, *Gomorrah,* on the Neapolitan Mafia, the Camorra, and believe me, the Sicilians pale into benign players by comparison.)

Southern Italy and Sicily sent their poorest to the US, and among them were the Mafiosi of Corleone and other depressed areas of the country. But why today, with EU money pouring in, with tourism on the rise? Why so many houses with shutters down, windows sealed shut? Mainland Italy sends huge subsidies to Sicily—for the 3,000 people employed to protect forests in the Piedmont, there are 40,000 on the island, we were told. Corruption is one reason, unemployment another. Illegal migrant labour from North Africa is employed on all the greenhouse farms, working for little money and in conditions that no locals would accept. And even the smallest town now has malls and supermarkets. Carrefour. LIDL. Conad. They're all here.

It's not for nothing that Sicily is said to be a country of paradoxes.

* * *

Dolce, dolce, dolce. Sicily must be the sweets capital of the world because you cannot imagine the varieties of scrumptious confections in its pasticcerias. With or without ricotta. With or without almonds. Marzipan. Chocolate. Candied fruit. Buttermilk curd. Light-as-air pastries.

Mouth-watering biscuits twisted around fig, cinnamon and clove confit. It was all those nuns servicing all those priests and churches who exalted pastry-making to a fine art. They baked and baked, they trained new initiates, as well as children sent to their orphanages and convents, and they left a legacy of confectionery that flourishes to this day.

In Erice, at Maria Grammatico's café, this art is found at its best and can be savoured to complete delight. Deposited by her poverty-stricken mother in the 1950s, at the age of eleven, to the care of the nuns of S. Carlo, Maria toiled tirelessly in the kitchens, learning the art of pastry-making in its smallest detail—beating sugar mixtures for six hours at a stretch, priming the ovens before daybreak—mastering it, and opening her own shop in the 1960s.

It was the same in Modica, where Casa Don Puglisi (a laboritario dolcario) was established by the nuns to honour the memory of the priest, Don Puglisi, murdered by the Mafia because of his work with drug addicts. All proceeds from the laboritario go towards rehabilitating former addicts and continuing Don Puglisi's work.

But it was in the Siracusa market, itself a gastronomic wonder, that we had the best sandwiches ever. You enter the market through bric-a-brac stalls, manned mostly by immigrants, past the small household goods, cosmetics and toiletries, cheap tourist trinkets and jewellery stands, the usual fare, and then, a cornucopia of fruit and vegetables! Giant cauliflowers and pumpkins, deep purple aubergines offset by ivory-coloured onions (some weighing a kilo each) and bright red and yellow tomatoes and peppers;

bottlegreen zucchini, slender and long; olives, olives and more olives. All the frutta del mare, fish and crustaceans, meats, sausages, hams, walnuts the size of small apples, and cheeses—stand after stand of the most delectable, fresh buttery-yellow or pale varieties. The aroma alone is so heady you can faint!

After savouring the smoked ricotta with olive oil and herbs at his stall, the voluble owner insisted we sample his daughter's sandwich. We demurred, having had our usual heavy breakfast. But no, you must, said Antonella. In we went to where his daughter was standing behind the counter, waiting to show off her art-of-the-sandwich. She took out a long baguette, cut it in half length-wise and then gouged out the bready part so that it formed little mounds. 'I say you in Eenglish,' she said, as she proceeded to sprinkle the baguette with olive oil. 'Now, oregano,' she went on, and picked up a sprig, crushed the herb and let it fall on the baguette in a flurry of tiny flakes. 'Then formaggio, plenty of it, and prosciutto,' and turning, she cut the thinnest slices that you could almost see through, laid them on the cheese, placed the other half of the baguette on top, pressed it down, and cut eight equal pieces. The combination of flavours and the freshness of the ingredients made for a taste I can still conjure up—and she wouldn't accept a penny for it.

* * *

Etna. Stromboli. Vulcano. Still smoking and spewing out lava and gases, still able to uproot people and scatter rocks, burning hot, across the land. And yes, weirdly, still have people skiing down their snow-clad slopes in winter.

Unlike the small volcanic rocks that disappear into the landscape, the boulders that rise up into the air across the island are like hills, craggy and porous, beautiful formations, material for the amphitheatres and pavilions and stadia built by the Greeks and Romans. Vast vistas we saw on the way from Agrigento to Segesta in the west, green and cultivated, yet brooding. Albeit a sunlit brooding. The countryside is of arresting beauty and isolation. You can go for miles without seeing any signs of habitation or cultivation, then suddenly a mini-forest of succulent cacti, laden with dusky pink prickly pears appears, lining the rock-face. Jasmine, wisteria, brilliant bougainvillea, resplendent against church façades; white, pale pink and scarlet oleanders against a sky so blue, it's blinding. The terrain dips and rises, woods appear and disappear, and always those lowering rocky hills in the background. At night nature comes into its own in this landscape, timeless and enigmatic.

Time. And in its interstices, history. Greeks. Phoenicians. Romans. Carthaginians. Arabs and Ottomans and Spaniards, they've all been in Sicily, they've all left their footprints on it. It's only today that we think of history and culture as being enclosed and self-contained; in Sicily (but elsewhere in the Levant, too) both have been criss-crossed in so many complex ways as to defy reduction, to remain richly and tantalisingly layered.

It's always seemed to me that there are more Greek ruins

outside Greece than in it, so it was no surprise to find that the most perfectly preserved Greek temple is in Agrigento, a coastal town in south-western Sicily. The temple of Concordia perched on a hilltop, perfectly proportioned, its thirteen Doric pillars intact. Preserved because it was converted into a church in 600 AD by Bishop Grigoriodelle Rape, then restored in the eighteenth century. But no matter how hard I tried to cast back in time, I couldn't imagine it in 430 BC, which is when it was built. So many thousands of years, so much worship, such splendour. In the foreground an 800-year-old olive tree, still bearing fruit, and also in the foreground, a most stunning bronze sculpture made as recently as 2011 by Hungarian sculptor, Igor Mitoraj, of the fallen Icarus. Broken wings, shattered legs, lying on his side, but with the most beautiful face in repose that I have ever seen. Of such surpassing beauty as to be god-like.

Also lying on his side and magnificent in its scale, is a statue of Apollo that was in a temple, now in ruins, on the eastern edge of the complex. In some ways reminiscent of those gigantic fallen statues in Luxor, unimaginable as fallen gods, the power and the glory vanquished by time.

So many temples of sublime and lofty near-perfection on the island, and the one in Segesta, nestled in verdant forest, we could almost see from our terrace at Tenute Pispisa. You rounded a curve on the hill road and there it was, supreme and magnificent in its isolation. You think, when you're climbing up the hill to it that it will reveal itself in stages—massive base, then sections of its columns tapering up to their capitals, and finally the crowning pediment—but no. It hits you smack between the eyes the minute you reach the top, and rises up majestically, sky above and wooded hills all around.

Splendid as they are, I couldn't help thinking that the temples at Karnak and Luxor, built a good couple of thousand years earlier, had already scaled all heights of grandeur and imagination and aesthetics. What then, is so extraordinary about Greek temples? 'Theorised aesthetics for western civilisation,' said Pogey, which didn't seem reason enough to me to judge them superior. We agreed to disagree. We stayed till the sun went down and darkness stained the sky, the trees and hills became a smudge first, and then, in a kind of surreal movement, seemed to be drawn into the temple precinct itself as night fell slowly.

For some reason, the Greek ruins at Selinunte affected me much more deeply, perhaps because the site really is in ruins. In one particular complex of three adjoining temples, only one was still standing (just about), most of its columns gone, a few in halves, only the bases more or less intact. The rest was left to the imagination. And next to it were great mountains of rubble—enormous remains of pillars and pediments and capitals, piled one on top of the other, as if felled by the swinging of a giant Brobdingnagian pendulum. Lying there in front of you, the huge size and weight of the stones are staggering; here, now, we could gauge more accurately, and immediately, the propensity of this earthquake-prone area to reduce everything to rubble.

Time.

We thought, when we left Segesta for Palermo that, really, we had seen everything now, seen the soaring cathedrals and churches, the Greek amphitheatres and Roman stadia, the palazzos and castles and the magnificent mosaics of Piazza Armerina; we thought in Palermo we would unwind, recollect it all in tranquility…Eat good food, wander along the coast, linger in the markets. We did all that, of course, but we had reckoned without Monreale and Capella Palatino and Chiesa Cataldo and the Matrice at Erice…and the mosaics!

I mean, it isn't as if we haven't seen mosaics. Istanbul, Ravenna, Venice, Damascus, but the wealth and extent of them in Sicily is something else. At the Villa Romana del Casale, near Armerina, we saw what must be the largest expanse of secular mosaics in Europe. Every inch of floor in every room it seemed, had been decorated with scenes of extraordinary detail and depth. Myth and conquest, fable and fantasy; tales of valour and glory, hunting and fishing, feasting and jousting. Medallions and borders, heraldry and pennants, sport and leisure activity—every aspect of life and living depicted, all in the span of twenty years, from 286–305 AD.

The villa was the country retreat of Marcus Aurelius, built when he was co-emperor of Rome, with Diocletian. The villa itself is enormous, a little city almost, with 3535 sq mt just of floor mosaics! After a twelfth-century landslide it was submerged under mud for 700 years, which of course, is why it's so well preserved. Nevertheless, it needed a massive and sophisticated restoration programme and was closed for many years, opening for visitors only in 2010 or so. Restoration work continues, but the Great Hunt, a 64-metre floor mosaic can be seen in all its splendid beauty. The hunt was a great Roman sport, and the story here is the hunting of wild animals in North Africa by the Romans, and their transport across the sea to Rome. The skill of the draftsmen was exceptional and the colours—my goodness, the colours! Glowing with a subtle radiance even in the dim light of the interiors; where natural light was brighter, they fairly leapt out at you and filled your eyes with their magic. I have really never seen such fluidity and movement in animals poised for flight or tensed for attack, nor faces of such mobility and animation, in stone. In chips of stone, what's more.

But then we saw the mosaics in the Capella Palatina in Palermo, and agreed that never before had we seen religious mosaics of such dazzling brilliance, as here. Not in Ravenna, nor in Istanbul, not in Damascus either. Even Venice. Walls and vaults and altars and domes, covered with the story of Jesus and every Biblical tale and miracle. And on the floors—geometric designs that are such a clear reference to Islamic art and its influence, such a graceful, abstract incorporation into the richly figurative narratives on the rest of the surfaces, that you had to applaud the eclecticism of the duke who built it. Indeed, one legend has it that he was part Muslim, and a delicate mosaic mihrab in one alcove would seem to corroborate this. But who knows? Well, we looked and looked and couldn't stop till we had aching necks and leaden feet and could look no more, at least till the following morning when we saw more, oh very much more, of the same at the Cathedral and Cloisters in Monreale. Here too, the gilded and burnished mosaics gleam and glint in the half-light of the cathedral, here too, abstract arabesque designs adorn the floor and little pillars in alcoves and niches. And whether or not craftsmen were imported from Turkey, a certain whimsicality peeks through some of the depictions—Adam, reclining on one side as Eve emerges from his rib, looks distinctly put out, and Eve, reaching for the forbidden fruit is egged on by the serpent: 'No! You will not die! God knows in fact that on the day you eat it your eyes will be opened and you will be like gods, knowing good and evil.'

It was almost a relief to return to the heaving, pulsing street life outside our little hotel in Palermo. Beautifully converted stables that were part of one of the city's numerous palazzos, located on Porta del Castro (after Fidel) in the old town. You stepped out and were immediately engulfed by the everyday life of the locals, exuberant and unselfconscious. The best 'antidote' to Monreale was our local market which never slept! We discovered many local delights—Sicilian pesto, for instance, is quite different from the Ligurian, with pistachios and almonds instead of pine nuts. Divine. And arancina, like a rissole but made with rice, not potatoes, stuffed with mince—or ricotta and spinach, or ham—and deep fried. Dee-lish. Pogey couldn't have enough of the orrata, sea bream, coated liberally with sea salt, lemon and herbs and grilled; Jon OD'd on spaghetti Norma and I thought all the antipasti were simply wonderful, but especially the aubergine caponata! Pickled, sundried tomatoes with ricotta, aubergines in olive oil and herbs, prosciutto-wrapped olives; fingerlings....

Better stop, before I feel faint with hunger for all of them!

Bergerac and the Dordogne Valley: Wine, More Wine—and Noble Rot

June 2005

Everyone said, 'Oh, how wonderful!' when we told them we were going on a two-week holiday to Bergerac and the Dordogne Valley. 'Beautiful country, marvellous food and wine…'—which is, of course, why we chose to come here in the first place! The Dordogne is wine country, the heart of the Bordeaux and Saint-Émilion vineyards, and the great chateaux of French wines; plus the petit vins or more modest wines of the Bergerac region. *Plus*, we were told, the cuisine of south-west France is also famous for its duck, foie gras, walnut oil and cheeses.

The four of us, Madhu, Krishna, Pogey and I, were all set for a fortnight of wine-tasting, gourmandising, and meandering along the Dordogne, stopping at a chateau or two, savouring the countryside, unwinding and stretching out in Cause de Clerans, at Martin and Margaret Miles' place—a twelfth-century house and tower which has been in English ownership for the last hundred years.

In addition to duck and wine and foie gras, this is Eleanor of Acquitaine's corner of France, as well as of

The House at Cause de Clarens

Montaigne (who wrote his *Essays* nearby), Cyrano de Bergerac, Marguerite Duras (who took the name of the town of Duras as her nom de plume), and—a far cry from them all!—the famous Josephine Baker of the Folies Bergère. She was the other kind of American in Paris in the 1920s and '30s, a young black girl from St Louis, dirt poor, but with a beautiful body and a gift for dancing, who arrived in Paris and became the darling of the demi-mondaine, habitués of Montmarte's night clubs and casinos. Yes, she had lived in the Dordogne, too.

We left Paris on Monday, 6 June, on the TGV railway line to Bordeaux, then the local train to Bergerac, from where we picked up our rental car and drove 8 km to Cause de Clarens. It was an unprepossessing start. As we peered out of the train windows, the sky grew a darker and darker grey the further south we travelled, and the countryside wasn't much better. Long stretches of industrial estates and new construction, the blight of many modern towns and cities. Occasionally, an expanse of wooded farmland—but not much more than that. Is this what everyone was going on about? Perhaps it would open up suddenly, closer to Bordeaux. We certainly hoped so. But Bordeaux to Bergerac was, if anything, even more disappointing. Oh, there was countryside all right, and now miles and miles of vineyards with wooded hills in the background, but not quite what I had expected. Did I imagine something of Provence, perhaps? An expanse of wild flowers, rolling fields, a softer, more Italian landscape? My mistake. This was France, and wine country, but nothing like Tuscany, the other wine-growing region we had spent a couple of weeks in a few years earlier.

The Miles' house—Tour Anglaise as it's known to the village—is utterly charming. Two hundred years old, set in the shadow of the Tower and looming dungeon, surrounded by a wild garden, old stone walls through which grow ivy and creepers and rose cactus, but comfortable and welcoming inside. Full of light and air, wonderful views, alive with birdsong, and oh, such sweet-smelling air. We had taken the house, not the Tower—also very imaginatively converted—and our bedroom overlooked one side of the garden with walnut, cherry, nectarine, apple and peach trees, and wild roses. Lovely. And a stream running alongside. That evening, we cooked our first simple meal at home and sampled a local Bergerac wine (ordinary), then called it a day.

The next morning Madhu, Krishna and Pogey went for a short morning walk, then came back, and over breakfast pored over all the pamphlets and *Rough Guides* and *Michelins* to decide what our plan for the day would be. This part of the Dordogne is known for its bastides, or fortress towns, and the Lascaux caves. We decided we would go to the fort towns of Beynac-et-Cazenac, then to Sarlat, a medieval town about 75 km away.

Beynac is a charming citadel perched on the Dordogne, a hill town of lovely little stone houses and steep, narrow lanes. Too steep for Madhu and me, so we stayed at mid-level while Pogey and Krishna went to the top to see the church and chateau. Unremarkable, was their verdict, except for the panoramic view. We debated about whether to take a river cruise or see the other chateaux along the river, then decided against—the middle of the afternoon wasn't such a good time for a trip down the river!

After a pleasant lunch at a restaurant on the river (although I ordered disastrously! What I thought would be fried shrimp turned out to be very clawy crayfish, practically inedible), we made our way to Les Milandes, Josephine Baker's chateau set in 300 acres of parkland. It was a glorious afternoon, balmy and mild, not a cloud in the sky. The kind of day that makes you happy to be alive.

There was a display of falconry on at Les Milandes when we arrived. Terribly sad to see those magnificent birds chained to their posts, especially after you've watched them soar up in flight, wheeling and swooping in the sky, but unable to fly any further than their custodians allow them to. A paean to unfreedom.

When Josephine Baker first performed at the Folies Bergère in Paris, among her audience were Charles de Gaulle, Ernest Hemingway, Edith Piaf and Igor Stravinsky. Her long line of lovers and husbands included the Crown Prince of Sweden and Georges Simenon, and she moved around with the likes of le Corbusier and other illustrious Parisiennes. The chateau is filled with photographs of her in the nude, embellished with nothing but feathers and plumes, the body of a woman permanently on display, the ultimate white male fantasy of a black Venus or a black Athena. Yet here was a woman who was intuitively political: during the war she was part of the French Resistance;

after she bought Les Milandes in 1947 and added those hundreds of hectares to it, she threw it open to the local inhabitants, running the whole estate as what she called a 'village du monde', a multicultural community. Unable to have children of her own, she adopted a dozen babies from all over the world and brought them up in Les Milandes, a truly rainbow tribe: 'My children have proved that there are no more continents, no more obstacles, no more problems to prevent understanding and respect between human beings, no more excuses that colour and religious differences prevent unity…My dream is universal brotherhood, a dream I have realised at Les Milandes,' she said.

This was much before the era of flower children and hippie communes and rainbow coalitions, yet Josephine Baker died a pauper; one of the most heartbreaking photographs in the chateau is of her sitting on its steps, surrounded by cartons of her worldly belongings, trying to stop Les Milandes from being auctioned to pay her debts. This was the same Josephine who worked and worked in the theatre in order to pay for the chateau's upkeep, and for the children she rescued. What happened to all those children, I wonder? Where are they now?

I left the place feeling unutterably sad, why I don't know. One can't feel sorry for Josephine Baker, and yet…

We left Les Milandes and drove to Sarlat, a medieval town with cobbled streets, boutiques and tourist fare, rather like medieval tourist towns in many European countries. We would have lingered and wandered around some more, but Pogey declared that Sarlat 'simply doesn't have that lived-in feeling of Italian hill towns,' and started making tracks. Since he was driving us back, we really didn't have much choice. Anyway, it was almost 6 p.m. and we had a two-hour drive ahead of us. Plus we were eating at home, which meant cooking.

So, where was all that marvellous south-western French cuisine we were going to gorge on? So far, both food and wine had been trés ordinaire.

Acquitaine. That's what the Romans called this region, a land of waters. Each tributary of the Dordogne flows through its own regions and towns. At the time of the French Revolution, according to James Bentley, three cities were considered to be the capitals of the Dordogne: Perigod, Sarlat and Bergerac, each one serving as the capital for a year. Perigod began the cycle and remains the capital to this day. There are chateaux and castles all along the Dordogne, numbering well over a thousand, built mostly during the Hundred Years War, to protect their owners and the villagers around. Ever since Eleanor of Acquitaine married Henry Plantagenet, the French and the English have fought over the Dordogne.

In 1866, the district of Dordogne had 96,000 hectares of land under vine cultivation. In that year, the pest *Phylloxera aphid* attacked the young vines and killed them. The insect feeds on the sap of young vines, and in 1854, it reached the Midi by way of the Gironde river and arrived on the Dordogne. Wine production in this region has never fully recovered from the *Phylloxera aphid*. By the end of the 1800s, the wine-growing area had been reduced to just 31,000 hectares, and even after fifty years, in the 1950s, it increased only to about 36,000 hectares.

Caroline, the Miles' friend who lives close by, suggested we visit her brother's vineyard in Saint-Émilion (her father was/is a wine importer in Canada), and we decided to do just that on our next available free day!

The following day was given over to domesticity. The weekly market at Bergerac on Wednesdays is where we spent the morning and I foolishly bought three uncut, beautiful rubies—for an exorbitant €30! From India! But they were most unusual and irresistible. Krishna went overboard, as usual, buying fruit and vegetables, we got some lovely local cheeses and herbs and fresh stuff which smelt wonderful...

Afternoon was spent on laundry and ironing and writing and reading. Krishna made a very good ratatouille for dinner and we drank too much wine, also as usual.

Collapsed into bed at midnight in a state of complete contentment.

Pogey's birthday, 9 June. The day dawned bright and clear, as they say, and sitting out in the garden for morning tea with the sunlight slanting on the Tower and dungeon, birds high up in the sky, the rustle of leaves in the light breeze—it was glorious.

Hard though it was to tear ourselves away, we decided to make a trip to the caves at Lascaux or Lascaux II, as the ones you can visit are called—the original caves have been closed to the public (by André Malraux when he was culture minister) since 1968.

All the prehistoric caves in the Vezère Valley are clustered around the towns of Montignac and Les Eyzies, home to the greatest concentration of prehistoric sites in the world, and a UNESCO World Heritage Site. The Vezère Valley lies west of the town of Sarlat, itself east of Bergerac. A pleasant drive, the countryside continues to be less than spectacular, but it sort of grows on you—when it's not punctuated by modern commercial construction, that is. France is clearly more prosperous than middle Italy, and in fact, the one thing that strikes you so forcefully about all the hill towns here is how bourgeois they are, how spruced up, how few people you see on the streets. The nice thing about our village, Clerans, is that it's visibly old and lived in. Nothing dressed up about it. The ruins are ruins, old houses look old, the local pub is frequented by locals, it's a bit like an old shoe—comfortable and unpretentious. And, of course, everything closes from 12–2 p.m. That's rather nice, actually, everyone's much more relaxed around the south of France.

So, Lascaux II at 2 p.m. The caves themselves are a bit of a 'bizarre phenomenon', as James Bentley says, a faux recreation of something stupendously ancient, defying all the rules of the aesthetic and conservation canons. And, actually, it is a bit disquieting to walk down into a fibre-glassed pit with slick visuals telling you the story of how the caves were discovered; to experience the marriage of high technology and prehistory at such close quarters. Once you enter the caves, however, and look at the staggering drawings in the Hall of Bulls and the Axial chamber, you can't help being overawed. To see something like these drawings done 17,000 years ago up close (well, actually, the ones you see were only done twenty-five years ago, but there's a willing suspension of disbelief because you know you can't see the real thing, anyway), to feel the electric energy and dynamism of those great bulls—auruchs, they're called, ancestors of contemporary bulls—and stags and bisons...And the colours! Deep warm reds, ochres, charcoal black on cream-coloured limestone above you and all around you, to be encircled by 'hunting magic' as it's called—bizarre, but awe-inspiring at the same time. No one quite knows what these caves are about: ritual spaces? Shelters for a nomadic people? Propitiations? Whatever they might signify, they demonstrate extraordinary imagination and skill—or rather, artistry and skill because they're very realistic—and knowledge of colours.

It was too short a time that we spent in the caves but we came out humbled, even though Pogey the sceptic wondered how 'authentic' such an experience could be!

Evening was topped off with a really good meal at a local restaurant, Relais St Jacques, which lived up to all our expectations. Madhu and Pogey had all the regional specialities—ballotine, duck, local cheeses—I had a wonderful fish cooked in the most delicate sauce, very delicious, and a perfectly wonderful dessert: a flaky apple pie of a kind I'd never had before, topped with a burnt orange crust with ice cream. Yum.

In 1999, the département of Saint-Émilion was declared a World Heritage Site by UNESCO, in acknowledgement of its importance as a premier wine-growing region in the world. The entire place is dotted with small family chateaux with holdings of 8–12 hectares, and larger more famous co-operatives and family-held vineyards like Lafite, Mouton-Rothschild, Monbazillac, Pecharment and others. The Saint-Émilion wines are primarily Cabernet Sauvignon and Franc, and Merlot among the reds and rosés, and Semilion, Cabernet Blanc and Muscadelles for the sweet whites. The whites are much too sweet for my liking, they're mostly dessert wines, anyway, but the reds are good, and some of the ones we tasted were rather special. But as Montaigne said, 'If you make your pleasure depend on drinking only good wine, you condemn yourself to the pain of sometimes drinking bad wine. We must have a less exacting and free taste. To be a good drinker, one must not have too delicate a palate.'

So we took our untutored palates off to Saint-Émilion and the first of the chateaux we had arranged to visit. Almost all of them require you to book in advance, and some of them charge a small fee, which they usually waive if you buy some wine from them as well.

Here, finally, on the way to Saint-Émilion we drove through the kind of countryside you imagine for the south of France—vistas of vineyards, fringed by low wooded hills, a gently undulating landscape that stretches for miles around. Every few miles one of those fairytale chateaux rises up from the land, pointed conical turrets, ramparts, moats, a complete Disneyland fantasy.

We know almost nothing about wines in India (except

occasionally to recognise what we like or enjoy) so the sheer number of chateaux and their particular wines is astonishing. And that's only in Saint-Émilion. Then there are the other wine regions—Médoc, Graves, Margaux, Pauillac, Armagnac, Cognac, Sauterne, Bordeaux…the mind boggles. If we could manage even two or three of them and see four or five vineyards in each, it would be a real bonus.

Vineyards are almost always closed during lunch, so we wandered around the town of Saint-Émilion before going off to our first chateau. If the other little towns we stopped at seemed prosperous, Saint-Émilion is positively rich. Wine money. And everywhere you turn there's wine, wine and more wine. Wine museums, wine caves, wine boutiques, wine bars—naturally!—and the most beautiful array of wine glasses. Wanted to sweep the whole lot of them up. The central square, Place Pierre Meyrat, is exquisite: an old cathedral, the Eglise Collégiale, artfully restored, in warm gold limestone, a cluster of pretty buildings around, steep cobbled streets leading off from it into the town…Underneath its cobbled streets the hillside has been hollowed out (as in many other towns we noticed) to create Europe's largest underground church riddled with catacombs and quarries, ideal for storing wine. In 1152, Saint-Émilion passed into the hands of the British as part of the duchy of Acquitaine, but it has always been a self-governing commune.

Walking up one of the cobbled streets to the Place Pierre Meyrat, we stopped for our first wine-tasting in one of Saint-Émilion's wine boutiques. A couple of middling reds, nothing to write home about, but then the owner probably knew we weren't among the big buyers. For our part we were prepared to wait till the afternoon and our visit to Chateau Toinet Fombrauge, just outside the city.

Chateau Toinet Fombrauge

Charles Sierra, an amiable young man, runs their family-owned vineyard with evident enjoyment. He's originally from Spain but the vineyard has been in their family for over a century. Its 8 hectares grow a mix of Cabernet Sauvignon, Merlot and Cabernet Franc—the predominant grapes of the region, as we found on visiting other chateaux across Saint-Émilion, the Médoc, Margaux, Bordeaux and Pauillac. Except for Monbazillac, that is, which grows the Sauvignon Blanc for its very sweet whites. Allors, as the French would say, Charles showed us the pride of his vineyard, his 100-year-old Merlot vines, and told us that Chateau Toinet Fombrauge is one of only two 100-year-old Merlot vineyards in Saint-Émilion. But he has younger vines, too, and the best yield is from vines that are forty-five to sixty years old, when the roots go as far down as five to seven metres. Each vine should have a maximum of seven to eight bunches (at Chateau Palmer in the Margaux they [or rather, Celine] told us that they allowed no more than five bunches) to ensure quality, but it was hard to imagine that in just another three months the tight green beads that we saw on the vine would open into luscious, deep purple winking grapes. The Sierras' 40,000 plants—5,000 per hectare—yield roughly 40,000 bottles of wine each year, depending on the harvest. The two weeks in September–October when they harvest are a tense and tricky time because the grapes need to be picked at just the right moment. 'Sometimes,' said Charles, 'we have just one day for the Merlot, another for Cabernet Sauvignon, and after, poof! is over.' The grapes are then separated for the Grand Cru wines, and the regular classifications. Soil is critical for the Grand Crus, the best being clayey and gravelly, and each parcel of land has a different composition. Where you plant which grape—Merlot, Cabernet Sauvignon, Cabernet Blanc or Petit Verdot—is a matter of great importance, for on it depends the fate—and the taste!—of the wine.

'All my vats are concrete,' Charles told us as he led us into his 200-year old *chai* (cellars,) as they are known here. He has nine vats, and although empty now (the wine from 2004 having been bottled), if you look into them the walls are stained a dark wine-red, almost purple, and here, it's not hard to imagine the grapes bubbling and fermenting at temperatures of 28–30 degrees Centigrade. 'Some chateaux, they have steel vats now, but me, I prefer concrete because, you know, ze thick walls, zey maintain the temperature better.' Each vat takes 5,000–10,000 litres and the grapes ferment for three weeks. Then the thick outer skin is separated from the pulp and pressed separately, and three months later, blended with it, pressing for colour, aroma and balance. After this, it's transferred to oak barrels to mature for six to eight months. And even here, the grapes are selected and separated for each barrel because each wood lends a different quality and fragrance to the wine: cherry, vanilla or a nutty aroma; what may be perfect for the Merlot could be a big mistake for the Cabernet-Sauv, and of course, only French oak is good enough for the Grand Crus.

'Now,' he said, 'is time for tasting,' and taking a 200-year-old pipette he drew out the 2004 Grand Cru Merlot for us to savour. 'Not everyone gets to taste this,' he said, 'and after it's blended with Cabernet Sauvignon for a perfect balance, it's like an iron fist (the Cab) in a velvet glove (the Merlot).' We had to agree. The wine tasted wonderful, but he said, 'Best after ten years, drink it in 2014!'

Well, we couldn't wait that long and so we bought the 2000 Grand Cru, but as we were leaving, he gave us another of his Merlots 'to drink this evening', and with his compliments. We were completely bowled over, and not only by his generosity—he was so transparently in love with his vines that it was heartwarming.

A complete contrast to Monsieur Whatever at Chateau Laniote which we visited next. A showman to the hilt, he ushered us into his *chai*, switched on a slide presentation, whizzed through it at top speed, punctuating his commentary with poor jokes made at his wife's expense—oof! It didn't endear us to him any to see that his wine was really quite good—'I only do Grand Cru,' he declared, 'nothing else. But for me? I only drink wine from Pomerol, my wife's country!'—so we did buy a bottle. But we were in and out of his chateau in twenty minutes flat.

By now, we were reeling with all kinds of information we could make little sense of. Grand Cru? Cru Bourgeoise? First growth, second growth, premier classe, premier grand cru classe, second crus, third crus??

All we knew (more or less) was Grovers Red or White or Sula, or Madera, and if you were talking French wines, it was the downmarket Cuvées of sundry brands. On the rare occasions that we drank good French or Italian wines, they had usually been chosen by friends who knew what they were about.

More chateaux, more wine. Monbazillac Chateau and its vineyards sit beside a sixteenth-century canal, an old-style chateau with roundels and conical turrets, sloping vineyards, beautiful vistas—and the airport in the distance. The chateau has an interesting local history, having been the seat of the Huguenots, who were Protestants and maintained it as a bastion during the Wars of Religions in the fifteenth and sixteenth centuries. So the chateau itself is worth a visit, especially its wine cellars with their antique wine bottles, showing the evolution of the glass used for the bottles; but the wine is cloyingly sweet—practically undrinkable in my view, but undoubtedly, a superior dessert wine.

The sweetness, we were told, is a result of a particular fungus, *Botrytis cinerea* (or 'noble rot'—what a wonderful description) which causes the grapes to shrivel and release a distinctive sweetness. Wine-growers wait with bated breath for noble rot to set in. Monbazillac is famous for its sweet wines but my preference is for the drier ones; unfortunately, Bergerac is not really known for its secs (dry wine).

Sophie had already arrived by the time we got back in the evening. Sophie Baker, friend from long back, is a writer and gifted photographer, having done still photography for any number of British films. Married briefly to the actor, Ian Holme. Lover of India, game for almost anything! Pogey and Madhu rustled up a marvellous meal—a most delectable chicken cooked in herbs with a wine and cream sauce (Pogey); potatoes and cèpes (dried mushrooms, Madhu); haricot beans and a green salad. Strawberries and cream. Delicious. Sophie and I topped it off with a game of Scrabble which I won, although Sophie started off with a seven-letter word! Advantage S, but then I got the Q, Z, X, J and K, which sort of clinched it.

Then to bed, Donna Leone, and a deep and dreamless sleep.

Sunday morning was spent at the utterly delightful marché in Issigéac, about 10 km south of Bergerac. We spied a few of the same stall-owners here as we had seen at Bergerac, but the market was definitely much, much livelier and the town, quite charming. And, my God, what a mouth-watering array of fresh fruit, meats, cheeses, breads, herbs, spices…The man selling olives was especially nice, and his dried apricots and prunes and, of course, his olives were clearly well-known and loved. If only we could carry some of this back to Delhi, but of course, we couldn't. So we bought tarts and cheese for the evening, a Bergerac white wine and strawberries for the house, dried spices to immerse in olive oil and cèpes to take home with us. Better to savour it all here while we could—and we did! Oh, we have had such an absolute feast of food that we are quite spoilt forever.

The afternoon and evening were given over to Margaret and Martin Miles, who had just bicycled 1000 km from England to Cause de Clarens to raise money for UNICEF and autistic children. Margaret is a retired paediatrician (also the owner of the house we were renting) who is a passionate cyclist and has lived in south-west France for over thirty-five years, on and off. She had quite a reception in the village square—Sophie, all of us, her local friends who popped champagne to celebrate her feat. I must confess, I couldn't get all worked up about it. I mean, why the hell would anyone in their right mind want to cycle 1000 km for anything? Why not simply donate the money? But I suppose these things are a matter of conviction and passion, so why not? Still, I can think of better ways to spend my time and energy! Martin, her husband, is an interesting guy, a music agent who works with western classical musicians in London. So his clients are many of the well-known orchestras in Europe, he promotes artistes from all over, including Japan and India (Amjad Ali Khan only, so far) and—this will make Ratna happy—with Louis Langrée, the French conductor responsible for the Mostly Mozart Festival in New York every year. Enjoyed listening to his music CDs very much in the evenings whenever we were home.

Sophie left the next morning for her place in the Ardèche, and it all seemed rather quiet for a while. She has a way of animating spaces which is quite special. And because nature abhors a vacuum, we decided to fill it with—bastides. Yes. We would do a day of bastides, the fortified towns built variously by the French and English all over the south-west, to protect and defend themselves from each other during the Hundred Years War. We chose Beaumont and Monpazier, south-east of Bergerac and us. And, if we had time, the abbeys of Saint-Avit-Sénieur and Cadouin.

A light drizzle accompanied us on the drive to Beaumont, and the town itself was sweet but unremarkable, so we pressed onto Monpazier—which is absolutely lovely. It is the most perfectly preserved of the bastides in the region, a gem of a town with a perfect square. I think the most perfect square I have seen in Europe, St Marks in Venice apart. I mean, a square in a small off-the-beaten-track fortified town, nothing like Venice after all, but completely satisfying in its proportions, the arches leading into side streets, each house around the square, different, its doors and windows unique and special—just perfect. Perhaps because it was so unexpected we were utterly beguiled, and sat for a long time in the square, just appreciating its harmonious lines and absorbing its—yes, peace.

Totally unexpected in this medieval town of old stone and cobbled streets was a gallery of glass sculptures—we came upon it quite by chance, just off the main square, and it was breathtaking. Extremely good contemporary work, made with exquisite skill and imagination, everything from abstract to realistic…the two experiences, medieval and modern, both of such high quality and sophistication, were wholly unexpected, as I said, and completely satisfying.

After Monpazier (where we had an omelette lunch served by a young woman who was a Hollywood junkie), we made our way towards the abbeys, but both were disappointing. Monpazier is a hard act to follow in any event, but actually, having seen the Cistercian Abbey off Fountains Abbey in Yorkshire and, of course, Tintern Abbey in Wales, these could hardly compare. Besides, I was still mentally in the square at Monpazier.

THE MÉDOC AND ITS GREAT CHATEAUX

The following day we set off for Pauillac in the morning, via Bergerac, the car hire office and the phone shop, hoping to reach Pauillac and our hotel by noon, well in time for lunch before our 2 p.m. appointment at Chateau Mouton Rothschild. But we were quite late leaving Bergerac and then got hopelessly lost in Pauillac—just about made it to the chateau in time, but on very empty stomachs for a wine-tasting!

The Médoc is serious wine country, with chateaux positively littered across the countryside. Every time you turn your head, you light upon a name that was previously just a label on a bottle of wine: Chateau Latour, Lafite Rothschild (the French branch of the family), Mouton Rothschild (the English branch), Beychevelle, Pichon-Longueville, Margaux, Palmer, even the Barton and Guestier which every bootlegger in Delhi peddles! Picture-book chateaux with turrets and towers and neoclassical façades, very grand indeed. Serious wine and serious money.

By comparison, Chateau Mouton Rothschild is actually quite modest, even though it's probably the largest winery in Pauillac. But the Visitors' Centre and wine-tasting rooms and shop are like a museum. Beautifully designed, minimalist, trés elegant.

The year 2000 was very good for French reds, we were told, and this region—Saint-Émilion, Médoc, Bordeaux, Margaux and Pauillac—are famous for their reds. Eighty per cent of Mouton's 160 hectares grow Cab-Sauvignon, with Merlot, Cabernet Franc and Malbec making up the rest. Why reds and not whites? Because the micro-climate and soil, the air and water—what the French call 'terroir', which encompasses the environment as well as regional character—are ideal for it. Dry, hot summers, cold but not frosty winters, very little rain and a clayey, gravelly soil that is perfect for the Cabs. The stones in the soil heat up in summer, radiating upwards where the grapes hang low—they love it.

Wine-growing in France is strictly regulated. There's a ceiling on how much acreage can be devoted to vineyards, no irrigation is allowed, production is carefully controlled and, of course, the stringent standards of classification are rigorously maintained. The Grand Cru—or the first wine, as it is sometimes called—is the pick of the harvest.

It is in the heart of the Médoc that sixty great Crus Classés, 400 Crus Bourgeoise, 300 Crus Artisans and assorted others are produced. But among and within these the gradations are fine and numerous, so you have the Grand Cru Classé, the Premier Grand Cru Classé, the Crus Bourgeois Exceptionnel, the Cru Bourgeois Supérieur, and so on and on till the mind dizzies. But why would a single chateau's wines be classified so differently if they were growing the same grapes in their vineyards? Well, because each parcel of land, each hectare has different soil quality, which means that the superior grapes are planted on the better soils and consequently, produce better wine. As Sophie, who took us around Chateau Giscours said, 'Our wines are the best not because we're French or because it's the Margaux, but because of the soil.'

As important as these appellations, however, is the little legend at the bottom of the label that ensures the wine has been bottled in the chateau and not by wine merchants, who have been known to mix and match the wine that is delivered in barrels. So look for the line that says 'misenbouteille au chateau' or 'au domains'.

Every day we learnt something new.

In 1922 the young Baron Philippe de Rothschild, then twenty-two, came to Mouton and made the winery his life's work, and his passion. He modernised the cellar by introducing massive stainless steel vats into the winery and computerising temperature control for each vat. It's an amazing sight: row after row of huge steel vats into which the pressed grapes are fed for verification. It's sort of 'unnatural', the thought of all that fermenting going on in these clinical-looking containers, but that's where the grapes stay for approximately three weeks, bubbling and brewing (if one can use that word for wine), after which it's transferred to the cellars for maturing. I don't know, but somehow Charles Sierra's purple-stained vats seemed more like it to me.

Mouton is one of the two or three chateaux in the region with natural underground cellars, largely because the vineyards are on a hill (mouton) which makes them easier to build. The minute you enter the cellars, you're assailed by the heady smell of wine. Twenty-eight *enormous* oak barrels hold up to 22,500 litres each of wine—you can just imagine the scale—in cellars that are more than 100 metres long and 20 metres wide. Dimly lit. The wine remains in the cellars for two years (at a temperature of 14–16 degrees Centigrade) before it is bottled (so the 2004 harvest will be bottled in 2006), and the final three weeks of maturing takes place in smaller barrels on an upper floor (as long and as wide), which contains 1,000 barrels. Where each class of wine will be matured is a matter of careful analysis and selection, and the character and nature of each wine, or rather each barrel of oak, must be matched. Mouton uses only French oak (Sierra told us he's started using some Russian oak as well, but none of the wine-makers we met had had a satisfactory experience with American oak) and 50–80 per cent of its wine is first run Premier Grand Cru. The remaining 20 per cent is branded wine: this is wine that the chateau buys from other vineyards and matures and bottles at Mouton. The Mouton Cadet that I've always enjoyed is one of these, but they also buy wine from Chile and, lately, California. Despite its high-tech processing, however, some traditional practices remain: for the final clarification of the wine the preferred medium is egg-whites; when introduced into the barrels they cause sedimentation, and the wine that results is clear, limpid and brilliant.

Well, we couldn't wait to taste the wine! But before that we had to hear about the labels. In the 1950s, Philippe de Rothschild decided that a great wine like the Mouton Rothschild deserved a great label, and so he commissioned the greatest artists of the time to design them for him. Georges Braque, Marc Chagall, Niki de St Phalle, Balthus (whose 1993 label was not allowed into the US because he had been accused of child pornography), Keith Waring and many others designed for Mouton, and were paid in wine. Ten cases each, five of which were Mouton wines, and five from other chateaux. What a wonderful idea. The other wonderful idea the Baron had was to create a wine museum in one of his old cellars, no longer in use. He has a fabulous collection of Dutch tapestries on wine-making, quite unusual, and an absolutely priceless collection of wine goblets, pitchers, glasses and carafes from Greece, Persia, Turkey and China. Two wine cups from eighteenth-century China, in particular, in the shape of bulls' heads, were utterly beguiling—I'd never seen anything like them.

We staggered out of the museum into the wine-tasting room but the wine, from their 2004 harvest, was disappointing. Too young, probably, tannins too strong, could do with another five years of maturing, at least. By now, we thought we could begin to tell the difference!

Back to the hotel where our rooms had a lovely view of the estuary, sailboats in the harbour, calm water, a light breeze, all very relaxing. Later that evening we went for a walk on the pier, then ate at La Salamander, drank a Médoc red, and finally fell into bed, completely pooped. Wine-tasting can be quite exhausting!

In the morning we visited Chateau Siran, which was owned by the family of Henri de Toulouse-Lautrec till the 1850s, when it was bought by its present owners. It's a charming little (if 40 hectares can be called that) vineyard which produces about 150,000 bottles every year, 100,000 of quality Margaux, 50,000 of Haute Supérieur. Like Charles Sierra's this chateau, too, uses concrete vats for vinification because each grape variety needs to be treated separately—the huge steel vats don't allow that.

The trend for designer labels has obviously caught on because here, too, each year's harvest has its own label: 1989 depicted the Fall of the Berlin Wall, 1986 Halley's Comets, 1993, the French Paradox, and 2000 had a millennium label. But the chateau also has beautiful old maps of the Gironde region and a really interesting collection of wine jugs from all over, including His and Hers jugs, Jacques and Jacqueline! And its wine-tasting room was certainly the nicest we had been to, with a rare collection of hand-painted plates covering the walls. We bought a bottle of its Haute Supérieur, made a quick detour to see the stately Chateau Giscours, now owned by a Dutch supermarket king who also owns the SPAR chain in France. Then to a light and refreshing lunch in a small sidewalk café, with a full view of some more vineyards.

Wine-growing is so commercialised now that major corporations (who may have nothing to do with wine) have entered the market. The Dutch owner is only one of many including the Japanese, who now have a controlling interest in the Margaux vineyards. Chateau Palmer, a premier Margaux wine, is jointly owned by British, French and Dutch wine merchants, and has been in the business since 1856. It was our last stop in Margaux, and is well known for its elegant, feminine reds, Cab and Merlot. Fifty per cent of its production is Grand Cru, and the remaining 50 per cent of something intriguingly called Alter Ego. A wine by any other name is still wine, I suppose, but alter ego? 'It's a wine for today,' explained Céline who took us around, 'to drink now while you wait for the Grand Crus to mature. Hence, alter ego.' Ingenuous.

Across the garden, which you can see from the chateau's picture window, in its final maturing cellar is its chief competitor—the very stately Chateau Margaux, perhaps the most famous of the Médoc-Margaux Grand Cru-Classés. Even more remarkable is the fact that it is run by a woman, Corinne Mentzelpoulos, of French–Greek descent. She was just twenty-seven when she took over from her father who passed away suddenly, and in those days, the wine establishment of Bordeaux wasn't too welcoming of women. But there's more than one now, and they're all formidable. Baronne Philippine de Rothschild of Mouton Rothschild (recently deceased); Caroline Frey and Emanuelle de Aligny of Chateaux Lagune and Angelis, and Lorraine Rustmann and Nancy Bignon-Cordier, co-owners of Chateau Talbot, a Saint-Julien Grand Cru. The two sisters have a brand-new high-tech cellar and (as Nancy says) 'a relaxed yet extremely perfectionist ambience in the vineyard'.

We returned to Bergerac, tired but very happy, and after all that wine and duck and fish and foie gras, were actually looking forward to a simple vegetarian meal of pasta and salad. Which is exactly what we had when we got home.

Finally, a lazy morning—no rushing off to a vineyard, no driving, no rubber-necking. Since these were our last few days in Cause de Clerans we soaked up the balmy weather and elastic time, and just stretched out.

In the evening, Vishwanadhan, the painter, and his partner, Nadine, arrived from Paris and we opened the Haute Supérieur we had bought at Chateau Siran. Good, but not great. However Nadine had bought some wonderful cheeses on the way (they drove from Paris), which more than made up.

Sitting in Margaret and Miles' garden, sharing a drink—their son and his girlfriend had also just arrived—desultory conversation, the evening light waning, we could feel every fibre of our beings relaxing. Like being in a warm bath.

Martin decided he was going to take us to his favourite chateau in Monbazillac, to taste some real wine! It was all very well, these famous chateaux in Médoc and Saint-Émilion, but for a real wine-tasting experience, he declared, we had to accompany him.

He was right. (I was a bit sceptical, I must admit, because Monbazillac only has sweet wines, but he was right.) A short drive from Cause de Clerans took us to the Grand Maison, Monbazillac, Thierry Després' organic vineyard which has sweet whites, dry whites and some reds. Thierry's vineyard is planted with a high density of 5,000 plants per hectare, and is worked without any weed-killer or chemical fertiliser. This is a remarkable feat because it means very careful and vigilant grape-growing. All the harvesting is done by hand, fermentation and ageing are natural, and, in fact, his was the only chateau we visited whose architecture lent itself to natural processing. Most unusual.

All that organic viniculture must make a difference because Thierry's wines, all of them, were among the best we had tasted. Even the sweet whites. None of that cloying sweetness on the tongue and palette, just a light, fresh crispness that was utterly pleasing. Chilled, the wines would be, and were, absolutely delicious. And their names! Cuvée des Anges (of the angels) was one, simply heavenly. Here was a man—originally a banker who chucked it all up and became a wine-grower over twenty years ago—clearly passionate about his work, determined to hold his own in the face of corporate takeovers. Like Charles Sierra. In his wine-tasting room, crowded with cartons waiting to be shipped, old furniture, personal bric-a-brac, Pogey noticed a tapestry with a mountain scene hanging on one of the walls. Chinese, it looked like. Turned out that Thierry is a believer in fengshui, and the tapestry depicted the perfect orientation of mountain and plains.

* * *

On the way back to Paris, we stopped for lunch at Nadine's mother's house in Villaneuve, another bastide town, its walls, unfortunately, no longer there. Nadine's mother (who had a pet tortoise) gave us the most splendid meal we had had till then, in a lunch that lasted well over three hours! A sublime foie gras, local peasant specialities, a potato, peas and onion râgout, and the most delicately fried red snapper. Followed by cheese. Wine, of course. Sigh.

Well, this trip was nothing if not gastronomic.

At the Edge of Lake Coniston

England: Gardens and Lakes

July 2004

You can't be a student of English literature and not want to visit the Lake District, so when we got an offer to rent Joanne and Peter Eley's house on Lake Coniston, we took it! Decided to drive up from London through Yorkshire, stopping along the way whenever we felt like it.

Kettlewell, on the way to Coniston, was our first halt, where we had a completely satisfying day, which began most unpromisingly. Grey, drippy, pissing wet rain. At our Yorkshire breakfast at Jaynie and Michael Smith's B&B ('eat as much as you want'), we wondered glumly what we could do that was not in the rain. Pogey ordered a mostly Yorkshire breakfast of eggs, sausages, grilled tomatoes and toast (brown). Bunny had the same, minus sausages, plus bacon; I went vegetarian and had grilled tomatoes, mushrooms, baked beans and toast. Quite unYorkshire.

'Let's do Fountains Abbey,' I said, 'it sounds nice.' The most complete Cistercian Abbey in England. Roof blown off by Henry VIII when he took over the Catholic church, but otherwise in very good shape. Oh, he preserved the Water Mill because it brought in three pounds a year. Plus there was the Royal Studley Water Garden. Six hundred and fifty acres of them. Bunny and I are suckers for gardens, and 650 acres made our mouths water.

'But in this rain?' said Pogey.

'Well, what to do? It's England, after all, it may never stop, but we can't just stay in.'

He wandered off, post-breakfast, to call Charles Cockburn, an architect and conservationist, friend of some years, who used to teach at York. Now lives on a farm near Settle—which is the same Settle as the first Carlisle–Settle railway line, a historic first. Pogey knew him from all the Charles Wallace Fund Scholarships for conservation, having sent almost fifty students to York over the years. And I—funny how the small world map grows smaller—know him as the ex-husband of Cynthia Cockburn, the feminist researcher and writer. 'My London wife,' he called her. His Settle wife, Susi, suggested we meet at Harrogate for lunch. We knew Harrogate, we'd stopped there for dinner the day before, at a restaurant in Montpellier Garden. Beautiful town. Prosperous, too. 'We'll meet at one,' said Pogey, looking at his watch. It was almost 11 a.m. Still dripping.

'So, let's stop at Fountains Abbey on the way.' Bunny looked dubious, but good-humoured as ever, didn't demur. We set off. Bunny and Pogey in front, me at the back with my little nest of goodies—the *Rough Guide* to Cumbria, Malvern water, chocolate biscuits, umbrella, *The Guardian*, sundry maps, assorted jackets and jumpers.

Fountains Abbey lies east of Kettlewell, in a town called Ripon. Like the Lord, one of India's governors-general. We drove across the Yorkshire Dales, which must be among the most gorgeous landscapes in England. Formed by the Great Meltdown of the Ice Age, the Pennines were rounded by massive glacial movement. 'Dale' is valley, from the Nordic 'dalr' (Kettlewell is 'bubbling spring' from the same). Softly rolling hills, how-green-was-my-valley valleys dotted with sheep, it's also moorland, the famed Yorkshire moors of *Wuthering Heights*. The Brontës lived here—father, four sisters and Branwell, the brooding, tormented brother. Extraordinary, that when she died at twenty-eight, Emily had already written a masterpiece. And Charlotte—both sisters writing away in this windswept and in winter, bitterly cold and inhospitable weather. How did they do it? Of course, they all died young.

My thoughts wandered and meandered as I was struck again by the force of that enigmatic character, the mad woman in the attic, Rochester's first wife. How could Charlotte have thought her up? Such a tour de force. And Jean Rhys, whose *Wide Sargasso Sea* was another stroke of genius, the life of the first Mrs Rochester before she married him. And all the many, many interpretations and reinterpretations since. Jane Eyre's alter ego, Rochester's nemesis, everybody's skeleton in the closet.

Still raining. By the time we got to Fountains Abbey the sky was leaden and it was past noon. No time to cover 650 acres before lunch. But Jaynie Smith had told us it was supposed to clear in the afternoon, so should we try to come back, post-lunch? Well, we didn't really have a choice, so back we got into the car and headed off to Harrogate, fully expecting to spend the day at some mediocre art exhibition there if it continued to rain. Damn. If this is what it was going to be like at the lakes it would be a real shame.

We'd agreed to meet the Cockburns at Betty's Tea Rooms, famous throughout the region for her cream teas and cakes. Stumbling towards the restaurant under our umbrellas we spotted Susi in her red coat outside the door, but it was she who recognised Pogey. 'Charles has just gone to confirm our booking at a restaurant down the road,' she said, and as she finished speaking, he appeared. Silver hair in a ponytail, red suspenders, blue jacket. I might not have recognised him. He certainly didn't recognise me. 'Ah, it's all this ageing business,' he said dismissively, 'excuse me, dear lady.' Charles was seventy then. At the restaurant—'I'll have the crab thingummy,' he said—he informed us that he rises at 10.30, putters around till noon, reads the papers, has some lunch, naps till 4, reads again and waits for Susi to get home from work. 'I always thought I was pretty cool,' he said, 'but it's only after I retired that I realised how stressed I was.'

Like us all. Keep going till you drop. No time to stand and stare. I felt a twinge of envy.

A lovely lunch, punctuated by anecdotes of travel— theirs in Rajasthan, Kolkata, Delhi, ours in Italy, England, France—memorable encounters (in Jaisalmer for them, in Salisbury at Stonehenge for us), students and projects (Charles' and Pogey's), differences in conservation philosophy in England and India, modernity and how it travelled across time and space, print-making and map-making and making meaning of history.

'You must meet Cynthia, my London wife, in London,' said Charles as we said goodbye. 'Yes, actually, I've invited her to an event at Nehru Centre,' I replied. 'Ah, good,' he said. 'She's working on a book on Women in Black, you know.' 'I know,' I replied, 'I've been following her work for years.' He looked surprised for a moment. Then, 'Bloody women's networks,' he said, 'they're all over the place.' Looking up at the sky now warmed by a sun that had appeared as if on cue, he said, 'Go now, it's quite a trek at Fountains Abbey, but worth the trip. And call Cynthia,' he said, waving goodbye, 'it's her birthday next week.'

In the fading light of day (it was well past 4 p.m. by the time we reached), the old abbey with its pink-brown stone and soaring arches stood splendidly roofless, reaching up to the very heavens. The blue sky was its ceiling and at night, with the stars twinkling in the deep blue of its expanse, it would be magical. Old Henry could never have imagined that by blowing its roof off he would add immeasurably to its majesty.

Here, hard by Wordsworth country, I thought about Tintern Abbey, its purple stone glowing in the sun, and the long, long meditation it inspired in the poet. It's true, abbeys do do this to you as you wander through the monks' dormitories, the refectory, the Chapter House and great arched cellarium, arch after graceful arch, where 200 or more monks lived, worked, prayed and meditated. So many years of so much piety must surely seep into the stones and radiate out to touch those who visit now, hundreds of years later, far removed from the spirit of those times. The abbey is a skeletal vestige of its former glory but the power and influence of the abbots of yore are evident in what remains of its wealth and substance. No wonder Henry coveted the churches.

A long walk along the Skell river which flows through the estate, banked by thickly wooded hills, takes us to the Royal Studley Water Gardens, the only surviving example of a Georgian water garden. The river provides the theme for this unusual garden, which plays on the flow of water either in streams, as the river, or arrested in artfully designed still water pools, surrounded by uninterrupted expanses of green grass. No flowers, no pretty herbaceous borders, no superfluous ornamentation. Just a vast calm green water garden, reflecting the magisterial quietude of the abbey. So different from a zen garden, so similar in effect. The green enters your body, sticks to your ribs, induces the stillness of mind enjoined by all masters of meditation.

We returned to Kettlewell for dinner, a hugely delicious meal at the King's Arms. English pubs are no longer the steak-and-kidney pie places they used to be. Gourmet fare and wines are the norm now, and nouvelle cuisine, fresh fish and farm produce make for the most delectable dishes. Actually, we couldn't even finish ours.

We simply had to walk around the village after that Lucullan repast, and discovered that this sleepy little village had been the location for filming the famous 'Calendar Girls'. Good lord, how amazing. A couple of years earlier, the Women's Institute, famous all over England for their cakes and bakes, decided to raise some money for a cancer hospital. Big money. So they did the unthinkable for respectable Englishwomen—they posed nude, dressed in pearls and hats, behind fruit pies and strawberry shortcake and assorted pastries, and printed calendars of the photographs. They were a sell-out—I have one myself—the women raised a huge amount of money, and in no time a film was made on them. Bunny, who had seen the film, recognised several spots on our walk, and though there was a video of it in our room, by the time we got back we were too tired to watch it.

* * *

We drove all through the next morning to arrive in Coniston, at Lake End, Joanna and Peter Eley's house—or rather, converted stable—at the very bottom tip of Lake Coniston, the second largest lake in the Lake District. Much quieter and, in my opinion, more scenic than Windermere ('mere' meaning lake, so as the *Rough Guide* says, never Lake Windermere) and the Eley's place couldn't be more beautifully situated. They have their little stretch of beach (a euphemism for shingle and stone at the water's edge) at the bottom of their garden, a few boats and practically their own corner of the lake. Ringed by low hills, banks of trees receding into thick woods on the hill slopes—a little slice of paradise. But a pilgrimage to Grasmere, Wordsworth country, is obligatory. Later in the week, perhaps.

The view from the living-room in the Stable was straight out of the Romantics: soft green hills, a gentle sun, lambent air, birdsong. Bliss was in that dawn to be alive, and even though we're no longer that young, it was very nearly heaven. I just stood and stood in that early morning light, reminded of Ruskin's, 'There is no wealth but life.' What a gift to be here. To be able to walk out, down the path to the water's edge, look into its depths for hours, for a whole day, if one so desired.

But we had decided we would see a couple of gardens today, in the vicinity of Oxenholme, from where we were going to fetch Ratna (on the London train) at 1.30 p.m. Just enough time to do Levens Hall, a topiary garden in the morning, and Sizergh Castle and Gardens in the afternoon. Levens is a formal French garden in the English countryside, laid by a Frenchman, Guillaume Beaumont, gardener/designer to King James, who had also laid the gardens at Hampton Court. But England being England, successive owners and landscapists had planted avenues and herbaceous borders, some very English roses, and introduced a subtle informality in other garden features. The theme in the first of the enclosures was lilac and lemon, a colour-scape we saw in many other gardens as well. It made for a most pleasing harmony against the deep green of the topiary. Bunny and I were completely taken with the high topiary hedges, exclaimed at their branching patterns, at the artistry, which was revealed in a whole row of 'hollowed-out' hedges. Then Pogey told us how brutal and Japanese the whole business of training them to grow in these forms was, and we were silenced.

Some gardens fill me with deep longing. For settled beauty, for perennial regeneration, for lost innocence. Even for a kind of redemption. I suppose gardens are like temples, and tending a garden is a form of worship. Surely the simple perfection of nature, however ordered and arranged by humans, must fill one with humility and awe.

The rock garden at Sizergh came close. Not as grand as the one at Kew (and nowhere near as ingenuous as Muckross in Killarney that we saw in 2002,) but so complete in itself, so contained, that it radiated contentment. Pools of water and rock, burnt-red acers, low luxuriant ferns, pebbles, here and there some water-lilies, some cactus flowers, occasionally a cloud of pink or white blossoms—from the vantage point of a rock at a height in the near distance, the almost artless symmetry of the garden revealed itself in its balance of light and shade, mass and void, and palette of colours. I could happily have spent half the day there.

I can never be in a garden without thinking of May Sarton. In her *Journal of a Solitude* she writes about the absolute contentment of weeding, planting, re-potting and hoeing, the pure and simple therapy of gardening after a day's mental labour. She compares it to her writing which so often betrayed her with its contrivance, its stubborn resistance to fluency. Her garden, on the other hand, never failed her. If she gave it her best, it gave back a hundred-fold.

* * *

The next morning began with some agonised discussion between Bunny and Pogey on breakfast. Croissants? Toast with butter and jam? 'We'll do a proper egg breakfast tomorrow,' said Pogey, 'after Jon arrives.' Ratna was having her maple and pecan cereal, I was munching my toast. One croissant each for P and B. Then P spotted the Eleys' poached egg-maker and decided that was it. 'But we can't have poached eggs with croissants!' exclaimed Bunny. Well, put them back, then.

Poached eggs it was.

Thus fortified we set off for Brantwood, John Ruskin's home near Coniston. ('But doesn't he live in Mussoorie?' asked Ratna artlessly. 'No, silly,' we chorused, 'that's Ruskin *Bond*.' 'So how should *I* know?' she muttered.)

Brantwood ('brant' meaning high) is probably the most spectacularly located house in Coniston, with a panoramic view of the lake and hills in front, and densely planted woodland at the back. The art critic, designer, social reformer, writer and philosopher, John Ruskin, lived and died here, together with his cousins, Joan and Arthur Severn, in the last few years of his life. A Renaissance man in Victorian England, anti-capital, for the working classes, advocate of free education and a welfare state. Inspiration for the Socialists. In addition, a painter, essayist, art and architecture critic and designer himself. And a founder member of the National Trust, which acquired its first properties in this district.

In the last years of his life John Ruskin laid a woodland garden that covered a substantial part of the 200-acre estate. 'I am at work in my little garden amongst the hills, conscious of little more than the dust of the earth, more at peace than of old.' This was truly garden therapy, for Ruskin was recovering from a serious nervous breakdown in 1878. Extreme mental exhaustion, as a result of his unrelenting social and political (to say nothing of intellectual) labours over the past many decades. Brantwood by the lakes was his refuge, and it was here that Proust and Gandhi and many others visited him. In the room that he occupied before he broke down are poignant letters by him to friends describing his mental state, his favourite paintings, and precious objects—shells, feathers and such-like. After he recovered he never returned to this room. Extraordinary how eloquent a room can be, testimony to its inhabitant.

'Jumping Jenny' was the name of Ruskin's boat and it is now a tea room serving (as only the English can) scrumptious cream teas and light lunches. Warm sun, a stunning view of the lake, an egg and mayo sandwich, John Ruskin and Joan Severn's gardens before and behind us—bliss. Ratna and Bunny wanted to top off this feast with a pear and almond cake, but we decided to walk off some of the calories ingested first.

Joan Severn's gardens delight the heart. Or should I say, Bunny's and my hearts, because P and R thought they were much of a muchness. 'Ruskin was a fantastic man,' said Pogey, 'but all this—?' Ratna agreed. Well, Bunny and I are enchanted by most gardens, and these ones are remarkable for their colour. Quite different from the Professor's garden. Clear, true reds, deep, deep purples, brilliant yellows and oranges, pure white against all the greens of the woodland. 'Colour is a type of love,' Joan Severn believed, and her gardens, when she tended them, must have been a paen to that love. Her Harbour Walk garden, next to the daffodil meadow, is even today a beautiful panorama. 'All lovely things are also necessary,' she said. How true.

In 1848, Ruskin married a pretty Scottish lass who divorced him after six years—in fact, the marriage was annulled because Effie claimed that Ruskin was impotent. He challenged her charge but abandoned the case after a while, and the divorce came through in 1854. Funny, how all the laudatory claims made on Ruskin's behalf have elided all reference to his wife. We would never have known about her if we hadn't spotted Mary Lutyens' edited *Letters from Venice* by Euphemia Ruskin, written during the years Ruskin was working on his own multi-volume *Stones of Venice*. Pogey still considers Ruskin's writing on architecture among the classics—bought a copy of his *The Seven Lamps of Architecture*, in fact.

At 8 p.m., Bunny and I set out to fetch Jon from Oxenholme, but got a bit lost on the way back. By the time we returned at 9.45 or so, Pogey had cooked a delicious lamb stew with vegetables, which we devoured, followed by stewed plums and thick Jersey cream and then, to take wickedness even further, finished up with dark chocolate almond wafers that I had bought in Paris.

(Forgot to add that dinner was a riotous affair, with all of us noting how disapproving Prabeen [our mutual friend, a stickler for table manners] would have been of our table etiquette—no place settings, no proper cutlery, no napkins, Jon stabbing at his food with his fork and

Ratna saying, 'Kill the lamb, kill the lamb…' Most uncivilised.)

* * *

Bunny stumbled out of her room at 10 a.m. saying, 'Why didn't anybody wake me up?' Rhetorical question, really. Jon had been up for ages (at 10.30 he informed us that in ten minutes he would have been awake for four hours!), been to the lake and done his photography. So had Pogey. Ratna and I woke up around 8.30, and by the time Bunny descended for 'bed' tea, we were all showered and dressed. Shocking.

We decided to see some of the lakes—after poached eggs, that is. Ratna and Bunny pored over maps of the Lake District and, after intense consultation, announced our destination: Wast Water, in the west, via Elterwater and, possibly, Buttermere. Seeing as how it was already past 11, this would take us the better part of the day. Jon didn't mind—if we were out late he might be saved having to cook his famous spaghetti carbonara for dinner.

The weather didn't look too good, though. It had drizzled steadily all night and the sky was heavy with rainclouds. But onwards and upwards, we said, and fingers crossed. As we drove through tree-lined lanes along the west bank of Coniston Water (the opposite side from us), the landscape opened up in patches, revealing water and hills in lovely harmony. 'My God,' said Ratna wonderingly at one point, 'the clouds are really low.' 'A little bit of Prozac will take care of that,' Jon shot back, and we collapsed in giggles.

Kept giggling the whole way, more or less, because Jon was full of wisecracks. We hadn't been driving for even half an hour when he declared that it was lunch time and he was starving. 'But you've just had breakfast,' Bunny and I said simultaneously. 'So?' said Jon. 'How can you be hungry so soon,' I said, 'you must have worms. Have you got worms, Jon?' I asked. 'Why? You want some?' he replied.

See what I mean?

Not for nothing is the Lake District famous for its scenic beauty. There was not a mile of the way (highways apart, of which we took very few) that wasn't completely charming and, often, breathtakingly beautiful. And those villages with flowers spilling out of huge hanging planters, mullioned windows winking in the sun and post offices that were part of small family-run tuck or provisions shops—

We headed west and north from our place, passing through Skelwith, the Wrynose and Hardnott Passes, on higher and higher ground as we approached Eskdale Green in Langland Pikes country. Not far from Wast Water now. The Great Langdale is a U-shaped glacial valley over which tower the rocky Langland Pikes, the most arresting of the Lakeland fells. To get to Wast Water, the most isolated of the region's lakes, you cross the Great Langdale through narrow passes, through Great Gable and Scafell which, as the *Rough Guide* puts it, 'stand as a formidable last-gap boundary between the mountains of the central lakes and the gentler land to the south-west which smoothes out its wrinkles as it descends to the Cumbrian coast'.

The vistas are staggering. From the top of the Langland

Pikes the valley drops away, fold after fold of green undulating hills, forested and cultivated as sheep farms, as far as the eye can see. Standing atop any one of the hills, one is filled with wonder at what the Ice Age Meltdown wrought—geological and physical features of astounding beauty. We tore ourselves away from this rivetting landscape and continued towards Wast Water through the Eskdale Valley, among the prettiest in Lakeland. This is hiking—and biking—country par excellence, and even the farthest peaks had walkers dotted here and there on them.

The Pikes should have prepared us for the grandeur of Wast Water, but we were completely knocked out by its awesome beauty. What a lake! Remote, off the beaten track—in earlier times, according to Wordsworth, accessible through the Pikes only on horseback or by foot. It is the deepest of the lakes in the region, and the hills rise sheer and steep on one side of the slim and narrow finger of water before it opens out. It is a dark and brooding lake, the waters only slightly more fluid with little ripples, and this afternoon, an overcast sky added to its dark depths. There was no one else around in this isolated corner of the lake which Ratna discovered, walking down a narrow pebbly path overhung with rhododendron bushes. How spectacular it must be when they are in full bloom. We sat for a while at the edge of the lake, taking in its sombre splendour, looking down as the vista opened up; there was a temporary break in the clouds and the hills shone green-gold in the distance. Overhead, a passing cloud cast its lilac shadow on the next hill, and gulls called out as they alighted and took off from the tiny islet in the middle of the lake. Truly, in the words of the poet, 'No part of the country is more distinguished by sublimity.'

That deep longing came upon me again.

Reluctantly, we left Wast Water and continued northwards, to Derwent Water and, if there was time, to Buttermere. But would they compare with what we had just seen? Happily, each of the lakes is differently lovely. On the way we passed the pretty Bassenthwaite (thwaite meaning clearing) Lake and, very soon after, Derwent Water. From the road, which is on a high hill, the lake and its many islets was very pleasing but we couldn't linger—it was almost 8 p.m. already.

Jon cooked spaghetti carbonara for all of us, and a tomato/basil sauce for himself, followed by tomato and lettuce salad, and after that some rather delicious cherries.

A wonderful day.

* * *

Grey again. We could usually tell what kind of morning it would be by the light that came in through the skylight in our room. On a bright day, the room would light up around 4.30 a.m. and get steadily brighter, so that by 7 a.m. it was hard to keep the sun from striking your eyes. But today, even at 6 it was just a dull grey. Pogey and Jon had planned to go down to the lake to sketch and photograph, but abandoned the idea.

Mornings were usually relaxed. Tea, a chat about the day's plan, showering, a leisurely breakfast—we started out around 11.30 most days and today was no different. The Wordsworths, or rather Grasmere, was on the agenda. Whether we managed to do anything else depended on the weather.

Between 1813 and 1850, when he died, Wordsworth lived at Rydal Mount, a mile and a half south-east of Grasmere, overlooking Rydal Water—a small, quite exquisite lake just short of Grasmere. Although dark clouds had gathered and it looked like it would pour any minute, we decided to stop at the house, anyway.

The beautifully landscaped gardens (the English really have a way with gardens, and these were apparently laid by WW himself) drop down a hillside, and from the side of the hill where WW had his summer house, you can see Rydal Water glinting in the distance. The road below the house roared with traffic but in his time it must have been an idyllic spot. The Summer House is where WW wrote his poetry, pacing up and down on the terraced patch outside as he declaimed his lines. Across the Summer House is Dora's Field, a field full of daffodils planted in the memory of his daughter, Dora, who died before he did. An old, old sycamore, rhododendron bushes that must look splendid in bloom, rose creepers on the house—if this was the 'plain living' WW retreated to, it was pretty good.

I resisted going into the house itself, though Bunny and Jon did. The thing about a colonial education is that it opens up a whole area of experience but it also builds up a kind of rebellion against it. Having had to write tutorial after tutorial on 'Intimations of Mortality' and 'Tintern

Abbey', and read reams of critical writing on Wordsworth all during college, I just didn't want to know any more about his daily life with Dorothy, or read his letters to Coleridge. And yet, let's face it, my old desire to visit the Lake District surely owed a great deal to him and to his eloquent and moving poetry about it.

Leaving Rydal Mount we made our way to Grasmere, where Wordsworth lived from 1799 to 1808, in the famous Dove Cottage, a sweet, unassuming house less than a mile from the lake. But we stopped first at the Dove Cottage Café where we had our best lunch in the Lake District so far. Very good soup (me), sandwiches (P, R, J and B) and truly scrumptious scones. So good, in fact, that Jon ordered another round of sandwiches and Ratna, another round of scones!

Grasmere is probably the prettiest, and friendliest, of the lakes in the region. Small (relatively), dotted with islets, located almost in the centre of the village, it positively invites you to walk along it. If you do, you have one of the most pleasurable walks through woodland, along the banks of the lake, all the way around, for about three and a half miles. By the time we began walking, it was drizzling lightly and the sky had darkened. But the big bonus was that there were very few people around and it was almost as if we had the lake to ourselves. Now and again we came across another couple of walkers, also we felt, glad to be on their own. This was the only time we had actually spent a good part of the day at a lake, and even though it was raining, it was wonderful to stretch our legs and soak in the atmosphere.

By the time we started back to Coniston it was raining steadily, but on the way lay Tarn Hows, which is supposed to be quite spectacular. Tarn Hows is entirely man-made, on a piece of land donated in 1930 by Beatrix Potter, the children's book writer who also lived in the Lake District. The original owners enlarged two small tarns, planted spruce and pine, and landscaped the surroundings. The road to Tarn Hows is one of many tree-hung, winding country lanes that build up anticipation dramatically. When we reached the tarns, it was past 7 p.m. and we came upon a most amazing sight: low clouds encircled the hills around and thick mist enveloped the whole area. You could hardly see. We walked up a small hill in order to get to the tarns but stopped on top of the hill, arrested by what lay below. A jewel of a lake, its waters splintered by the falling rain, dark pines framing it, mysterious and almost preternatural. Amazing and wonderful to see the lakes like this when they seem to return to the elements, quite aloof from humanity.

The next day when we came back to see them in the clear light of day, they seemed to have lost their mystery. But then a shaft of sunlight through the pines lit up the waters to a crystalline blue, and it was magical again.

* * *

Jon decided he had had enough of the country, so we set off at 11.30 to drop him to the station at Oxenholme. Then, because we were more than halfway there already, we went up to Carlisle, the county capital of Cumbria. It's historic all right, but there's not much to see now apart from the Cathedral, a fourteenth-century Norman and Romanesque construction, and the old town and guild halls.

It was bright but *very* windy as we made our way to the Cathedral, nice enough but unremarkable except for two Norman arches (still preserved from a fire that destroyed much of the Cathedral in the sixteenth century) and one original Norman stained glass window, the East Window, inside. The rest are faithful nineteenth-century reproductions. Oh, yes, the organ pipes were rather grand.

Post-lunch we set off for Ullswater, the second-largest lake after Windermere, and in Wordsworth's opinion, the happiest combination of beauty and grandeur. Well, I must say, we were disappointed with the town end of it, so didn't linger long. But as we drove along its considerable length, seven and a half miles, we found a secluded spot and stopped—and were glad we did. Here we saw its full breadth, with an expanse of hills leaning against the sky, the lake spread out serenely below. At this spot, it *was* rather grand and beautiful, so we were compelled to agree with the poet.

Still, on the whole, a bit of a lost day.

* * *

Our last day in the Lake District. Bit grey, bit wet, bit sorry to be leaving (P, B and I, Ratna couldn't wait to return to London), but in an odd way, not really sorry to leave the Stable. We were all relieved that we would be in somewhat more salubrious surroundings shortly. The house is beautifully located, an absolutely marvellous space, but a bit unkempt. All that notwithstanding, we were really happy to have had the opportunity of staying at such a lovely spot, in considerable comfort.

Our departure was uneventful except that Bunny, who was driving, kept getting lost! Today, finally, the day we were leaving, we decided to go and see Blackwell House, a fine example of an arts and crafts house, now fully restored and open to the public.

If we could find it, that is.

After a couple of deadends, we managed to get onto the right track, and when we reached the house, on a hill overlooking Windermere with the most expansive, panoramic view of the lake and hills, we were really glad that Bunny had persuaded us to stop and see it.

Pogey thought he might sit outside and sketch, but it was so blustery—and, actually, quite cold—that he decided to accompany us into the house. And what a treat that was. Each room in this holiday home of Edward Holt—a Manchester brewer who ended up as mayor of Manchester (opposed stiffly by the Women's Temperance Union, who thought it most inappropriate that a brewer be lord mayor!)—has been lovingly and meticulously restored to present a whole of such perfection that one can only delight in it. Excellent woodwork, cabinet-making and marquetry, art deco stained glass, exquisite wallpaper murals and wood friezes, and spectacular views. The house itself was the work of Baillie Scott, and he made the most of its location. I've seen very few English homes that have the same airy and open feeling, filled with wood, but light and elegant and understated. The Arts & Crafts Movement in England was quite vigorous in the Lake District, and Blackwell has the best of contemporary crafts design on display. Glass, ceramic, leather and textiles—we were all completely taken with them.

On display was a special exhibition of the Anderson art nouveau collection of glass, ceramic and jewellery, a truly rich collection with objects of such artistry and exquisite craftsmanship that we were most impressed. I have such a weakness for art deco that I'm willing to be beguiled by almost anything, but this was truly special. I was particularly taken with the book covers—I wish we could do bindings like that, they would be so irresistible.

On the way out from the Anderson exhibit, we stepped into a little room on the side and found a most curious collection of black and white photographs in it. A gaggle of schoolgirls in uniform jumping over a gym horse, playing lacrosse in the garden, huddled around a dining table, in dormitories, grinning toothily in group photos…what on earth was this? Well, during and after the war years, Blackwell was a boarding school for girls, safe from the strafing of London, and the pictures told the story of that phase of Blackwell's history. On the window seat was an open book, recollections by old students visiting Blackwell now, of their time in the school. Amazing. Here was the school cook recounting tales of the girls; the student monitor; a teacher or two…what an archive! We could easily have spent a couple of hours leafing through the book, but it was time to go.

Imagine a great house like this surviving the ravages of a hundred-odd students!

All in all, a marvellous finale to a week of sheer joy.

www.ingramcontent.com/pod-product-compliance
Lightning Source LLC
Chambersburg PA
CBHW052049220426
43663CB00012B/2495